Latitude of Grace

About the author

Debbie Le Roux writes to explore the unseen forces that shape identity, love, loss and renewal. Her work is rooted in a belief that creativity and words can make sense of what life unsettles, offering both anchor points and new horizons. Raised in South Africa and now living in Australia, Debbie draws on landscapes of memory, resilience and belonging. Her writing often returns to the questions that matter most – how we endure, how we transform, and how we find our way back to ourselves.

In a career spanning more than three decades, Debbie has held senior executive roles across the education sectors of South Africa and Australia and now serves as CEO of an independent higher education institution in Sydney. Her career is marked by a commitment to leadership that sees both systems and the people within them. Beneath this lifelong commitment to people and purpose, however, runs an older truth. At heart, Debbie has always been an artist and a poet.

Debbie is a mother of two adult children who bring her great joy. She holds two master's degrees in Global Business Administration and TESOL, and brings to her creative work a reverence for learning, nature, art and the quiet architecture of human experience. Through poetry and art, she seeks to trace the tender cartographies that connect us, offering no easy answers but a hard-won grace. Her writing is a form of fieldwork – mapping the sacred in the everyday, and offering readers a sense of presence, possibility, and home. This is her first collection.

debbieleroux.com

Latitude of Grace

*Poetic field notes on resilience, becoming,
and the long arc of return*

Debbie Le Roux

HEMBURY
—BOOKS—

Copyright © Debbie Le Roux
First published by Hembury Books in 2025
hemburybooks.com.au
info@hemburybooks.com
Paperback ISBN 9781764055253
Hardback ISBN 9781764055246
Ebook ISBN 9781764055260

Compass icon designed by LittleFoxSVGDesign.
Every effort to contact copyright holders has been made. If you believe there has been an error, please contact the author.

The moral right of the author has been asserted.
All rights reserved. No portion of this book may be reproduced in any form without permission from the author and publisher, except as permitted by Australian copyright law.

A catalogue record for this book is available from the National Library of Australia

Contents

Notebook One: Origins 1
    Roots 2
    The Red Earth Knows 3
    Rain on Red Dust 3
    The First Drop 4
    Ancestral Heat 4
    The Naming Ground 5
    Cattle Fence Prayer 5
    Windmill Wisdom 6
    Anchor 6
    The First Yes 7
    The Kindness of Fields 7
    Burn Season 8
    A Fish Eagle Cries 8
    Line of Sight 9

Notebook Two: Love in the Margins 11
    Mother 12
    Love in the Margins 13
    My Mother's Daughter 13
    The Unfinished Script 14
    Uniform 15
    Her Bruises Were Invisible 15
    Fierce 16
    Mirror 17
    What I Would Say Now 17
    Sunflowers 18
    The Distance Between Us 19

    The Season She Died 20
    The House I Never Returned To 21
    Everywhere and Nowhere 22
    Fragments of her 23
    Love at the Edges 23

Notebook Three: Lessons in Light and Line 25
    Lessons in Line 26
    The Language of Looking 27
    The Eye Before the Word 27
    A Line that Believes 28
    Colour 28
    Study of Light 29
    Anatomy of Flight 29
    The Weight of a Line 30
    Palette 30
    Earthy Tones 31
    Brushes 31
    Lineage 32
    Negative Space 32
    Underpainting 33
    His Hand Over Mine 34
    Acrylic 34
    Horizon Line 35
    Composition 35
    Fugitive 36
    Drawing Life 37

Notebook Four: Fault Lines 39
    Tectonics 40
    Fracture 41
    Artefact 41
    Kin and Ash 42
    Pilcrow 43
    What I Keep Now 43
    Because the Moon is Still Here 44
    Elegy for the Unlived Life 44

    The Use of Small Things.. 45
    What the Wind Remembers 45
    Between the Lines... 46
    The Body Remembers 46
    Unfinished Things 47
    Some Days Are Wide 47
    Solitude.. 48
    A Practice of Staying... 49

Notebook Five: Milk and Measure 51
    Milk 52
    The Shape of Their Names................................... 53
    The Light She Keeps... 53
    Quiet Intelligence... 54
    Just Enough 55
    The Watch... 56
    Calibration... 56
    In the Small Hours.. 57
    All the Ways I Stayed 58
    The Leaving Begins Early 59
    Chapters 60
    Vow at Latitude Twenty South.............................. 61
    Quiet Strength.. 62
    Latent Geometry 63
    The One Who Loves Him 64
    Proposal at Forty-One North................................ 65
    Latitude Twenty-Seven South 66
    Widening... 66
    We Grew Up Together.. 67
    Their Laughter, My Home 68
    A Quiet Kind of Pride.. 68
    A Kind of Forever... 69
    Thread... 70
    Letter for Later.. 70
    Interlude 71
    Milk and Memory.. 71

Notebook Six: Salt and Bone 73
    Elemental 74
    Salt and Bone 75
    Seahorse. 76
    When it Broke 77
    The Exit. 77
    What Love Did. 78
    Remains 78
    Sediment. 79
    Antithetical. 79
    Portrait in Late Light 80
    Brink 80
    Another Way to Know 81
    After. 81
    Cairn 82
    Remains 82
    To Stay Human 83
    Reconstruction 84
    Hope 84
    Dandelion Woman. 85

Notebook Seven: Flint. 87
    Flint 88
    Spine. 88
    Dominion. 89
    Theory of Quiet Things 90
    Proof, With Paws. 91
    What To Do With Fire 91
    No Urgency 92
    In Praise of Enough. 92
    When It is Quiet. 93
    What Isn't Said 93
    Shear Line: A Theory of Stress 94
    Voice 95
    Assumptions 95
    The Law of Conservation 96
    Letter to the Self That Waited 96

    Holding the Line 97
    Learning Stillness 97
    Kindness Misread 98
    When the Blade Turns 98
    What They Don't See 99
    She Left Without Leaving 99
    Shape of Her Name 100
    Rite 100
    Threshold 101
    At the Edge of the Day 101
    Keys 102
    Script 103
    Heretic 104
    Bless the Unfinished 104
    The Game 105
    Bloodline 105
    Sacred Ground 106
    Undertone 106
    Archive 107
    Still, I Grow 108
    Night Watch 109

Notebook Eight: Latitude of Grace **111**
    Instructions for the Next Time You Break 112
    Resilience 113
    The Pebbles 114
    Compass 115
    Detachment 116
    From the Edge 117
    The Laws That Hold 118
    Contour 119
    Cartography 120
    The Quiet Room 120
    Tether 121
    Seismic Self 121
    The Shape of Grace 122
    Gravitas 123

    Paper Lantern 124
    With or Without Weather 124
    Half Light 125
    Uncorrected 125
    Uncharted 126
    Writing the Next Thing 126
    The Work Beneath the Work 127
    Inclination 127
    Equilibrium 128
    Sideways 128
    Laws of Return 129
    Meridian 129
    Golden Mean 130
    Tesseract 130
    Equinox 131
    Perimeter 131
    Caliper 132
    Laughter, Sums, and Stuff 133
    Fetch 134
    Anchor Point 135
    Continuance 136

Notebook Nine: Azimuth 139
    Florence 140
    Sovereignty 141
    Mosaic 142
    Absolution 143
    Dream Archive 144
    The Quiet Beneath 145
    Sanctuary 146
    David 147
    The Cartographer's Return 148
    Torso 149
    San Marco 150
    The Eternal City 150
    Marrow 151
    Montmartre 152

Sieve	153
Convergence	154
Customs	155
Provenance	155
The Language We Spoke	156
First Response	156
Contact	157
Risky Business	157
Euclidean Quiet	158
Even Then	159
Chiaroscuro	160
Intaglio	161
Flare	162
Longitude	162
Axiomatically You	163
Saltwork	164
Ratio	164
Arch	165
Grammar of Light	165
Palimpsest	166
Recalibration	167
Cartography	168
Joinery	168
Penumbra	169
Threshold	170
Stonefruit	170
Continuum	171
Echo Chamber	172
Index	172
You	173
Cutting Stone	173
Matriarch	174
Axis	175
Keel	176
Mercy	177

Notebook Ten: Singularity 179
    True North 180
    The Architecture of Joy 181
    Suture 182
    Cartography. 182
    Lexicon of the Hand 183
    Superposition 183
    Parallax. 184
    Particle and Wing 185
    Inner Physics. 185
    Vector Mind 186
    90° South. 187
    Finale: Singularity 188
    Epilogue 191

Dedication

For my children,
who made me brave.

For my father,
who taught me how to see.

For my mother,
who carried both fire and tenderness.

For the one who made gravity gentle,
and stitches laughter into every day.

And for the women who stay, who leave,
who learn to carry themselves with grace.

Special heartfelt thanks to my talented brother, Jade Holing, for generously sharing his exquisite photography. See more at jadeholing.co.za.

Alis volat propriis

She flies with her own wings

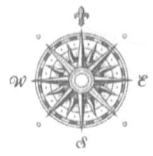

Prologue

Begin here:
in the quiet arithmetic of becoming,
each line drawn
between choice and consequence.

Fault lines form first in the sacred places
where bone leans into salt,
where ash thickens into marrow.

Not every break scatters.
Some carve new coordinates:
latitude drawn by what was lost,
longitude by what refused to yield.

Grace begins here:
in the silence that remains.

NOTEBOOK ONE
ORIGINS

25°49'44"S, 28°12'26"E

Field Note on Lineage and Latitude

Some things begin before you do. Before language, before memory, before your own name carries any weight. They begin in soil and story, in the scent of rain in the wind, in the voices of women moving through kitchens and courtyards like weather.

I was shaped in the quiet with light falling across tiled floors, by cautious hands that folded linen with precision and the fixed coordinates of a house that never shifted, even when everything inside it did. Girlhood wasn't something I stepped into. It unfolded around me, slow and unspoken, braided through heat and dust and the sound of my own thoughts in the dark.

These origins are not a straight line to a final destination. They are contour and crossing, latitude laid down in ritual, longitude carried in bone. Some truths don't speak aloud; they settle deeper, held in the marrow, where memory becomes instinct. Not everything that shapes you rises to the surface. Some truths remain underground and unsaid but deeply rooted. The things that mattered most in those early years weren't taught. They were absorbed, through scent, rhythm and the quiet calibration of feminine dominion - how a woman stands, listens, or walks through a room without asking permission.

What was given to me wasn't always explained. But it still lives in me as a heritage of bloodline, as bearing and pulse, as marrow and map.

Roots

We come from more than names.
We come from scent, from soil,
from the angle of light across a kitchen floor,
from a woman humming in Zulu
as she ironed our clothes.

Memory is not a straight line,
it lives in flint and pigment,
in the rhythm of water tanks,
and the way red earth
holds the scent of a storm
long before rain arrives.

This is a return to veld and voice,
to pigments stirred by instinct,
hands moving in knowledge
that cannot be passed down, only remembered.
It is a return to first prayers
murmured in a tongue I scarcely held
but trusted more than my own.
A return to girlhood,
barefoot and alert,
a young doe at the edge of the trees
tasting stories the wind
braided into my breath.
This is ancestry rooted in earth:
a pulse rising through dust and bone
carried in breath, remembered in blood,
a rhythm older than silence.

The Red Earth Knows

My feet ache for red earth fissured by heat
weathered skin knowing
the quiet wisdom of breaking,
its oxide dust rising
to mark each step with memory.

The angry elders gathered, thunder-thick judgment,
the sky rendering its sentence,
shouting a verdict:
a flash-wound that bled rain,
and the low percussion
of hope rolling through bone.

Mother Africa finds me barefoot,
her red dust rising to greet its own
lining the folds behind my knees.
She pressed silence into the arches of my feet.
I still wear the colour of her knowing,
a mandala written in the grammar of
belonging, veld and dust.

Rain on Red Dust

First rain.
That old, sacred smell of earth cracking open
drawing breath at last after winter's sullenness:
an exhale throbbing blood and memory.

I open the kitchen window just to feel it,
to let the scent in.
It's a hymn I still remember but no longer sing aloud.

The First Drop

Before the sky breaks,
there's a silence you can smell.
The dogs go still.
The air thickens dense with a secret.
The world holds its breath and then,
the first drop on a tin roof:
a sound older than language,
soft enough to remind me
what home feels like.

Ancestral Heat

There are women in my blood
who crossed mountains and veld fires
barefoot, returning home
still singing defiance in quiet revolution.

I carry their songs in my bones
some days I hum the tune
without knowing the words.
Their voices rise with mine:
unbroken and undeterred.

The Naming Ground

They gave me names before I knew how to answer.
Some were soft, some heavy as ox bone drenched in expectation.
But Africa knew who I was before I opened my mouth.
She tasted the salt on my skin,
read the latitude written in my bones
and whispered:
"She is not waiting to be named. She is already home."

Cattle Fence Prayer

The wire sags in the way old grief does,
a slackened spine of rust and dust,
weathered knots holding stubbornly
against the wind's playful fingers.
It marks the quiet border
between home and wilderness,
holding shape, offering shelter
to what remains.

Even rusted things
brittle and worn to silence
still carry the shape they once had,
hold their purpose in the marrow
leaning, even now,
into the shape of destiny.

Windmill Wisdom

Old steel rusting cleanly into its purpose.
Turning still.
Creaking truths into the blue silence
above the paddock
of meditating sheep and pensive cows.

She stands beneath it
arms folded listening to the rhythm
of something older than thought
a stubborn defiance
still moving through her bones.

Anchor

My grandmother didn't ask what I carried.
She just sat down beside it
hands still, eyes soft,
holding the silence
as if it too was hers to bear.
Only presence, rusks and coffee,
and the quiet gravity of knowing
some kinds of love
never need to be named.

The First Yes

I was shy then, quiet and unsure
how to be seen, but he saw me anyway.
It was autumn when I said yes
leaves trembling in their letting go.
He was my first certainty
not flawless, but full of the kind of hope
you only give once.
There was nothing hesitant
about the way we loved.
Even now, I honour that.
Some beginnings deserve
to be remembered without edits.

The Kindness of Fields

Some fields forgive you for not standing taller
than the swaying ears of wheat.
They cradle your fall without question
hold your weight without resistance
allowing you to unravel
and gently rise again.
I want to be that kind of field:
wide enough, to hold your quiet collapse
soft enough, to welcome you back whole.

Burn Season

The veld doesn't ask before it burns.
The wind carries flame across its back
like history it never meant to hold.
What survives blackens,
curls inward, then waits.
I come from this:
A place where fire is renewal not ruin,
where the ground writes its memory
in ash before blooming again
without permission.
There are scars in me
that smoke when it rains,
but I do not run from the heat.
I understand what it clears.

A Fish Eagle Cries

Three notes lifted from sky like smoke,
each one drawn through the lungs of the land.

The first- sharp, rising from the gorge
like something startled into flight.
It cuts the silence clean.

The second - open,
drawn wide across the belly of the valley,
where fever trees shiver in their roots.

The third - low, folding back
into the river's mouth,
where water keeps what the wind lets go.

Above the koppie,
the bird wheels against the sun's weight,
wings catching the heat's shimmer,
body still as stone.

The sound finds me before its shadow does.
It enters like a memory
I never claimed but always carried.

There are voices older than language.
Some echo through bone
until the body turns toward them on instinct, and listens.

Line of Sight

On the veld, there is nothing to break the view.
No shelter, but no hiding either.
My inheritance moves like wind
felt before seen, shaping the tall grass
in long, low arcs toward what came before me.

I carry those lines, mother to daughter,
bone to bone, drawn in stone and dust
lifted and laid down again.
This is how I know where I come from:
not by names, but by the way
the land stays open
long after anyone has walked it.

NOTEBOOK TWO
LOVE IN THE MARGINS

25°49'44"S, 28°12'26"E

Field Note on Love in the Margins

Not every kind of love lives at the centre. Some remain just outside the lines peripheral, but constant. They don't steer the course, but they shape the way you travel: the way you turn, the weight you carry and how far you drift before returning to yourself.

Some loves leave no bold headings, no declarations. They live in the white space of a life, tucked into footnotes, folded into sideways glances - a quiet presence that never asked for the foreground, yet never left the frame.

You don't navigate by these loves, but they alter your bearings. You chart more carefully when they're near and you learn to read the landscape differently. You learn to listen for what's unspoken, to wait for what's unsaid. You become attuned to inflection: the slight shift of tone, the change in the light, the silence that holds its own meaning.

It is not the plotted line that tells the story, but the margins and footnotes, the pauses, the almosts, the slight shifts that realigned your course. What seemed peripheral was already drawing the shape of the life that unfolded.

Love doesn't always claim territory. Sometimes, it marks the edges, not as absence, but as presence at a different scale.

Mother

We are born with coordinates already mapped into us
not just the shape of our hands or the timbre of our voice,
but the unseen lines of longing, duty and resilience.

My mother moved through the world with a kind of discipline,
drawn to structure when none was offered,
mothering with a fierce devotion that could hold or withhold.
And yet, she placed sunflowers in a vase
as if steadying the sun.

We lived on opposite sides of the world.
There were years we didn't quite fit into each other's days.
But even from that distance,
she taught me strength,
to take up space and hold the line
without conceding defeat.

She died in winter on African soil.
I could only return for the ritual of goodbye.
There's no house to return to - only memory,
and the quiet geometry
of how she lives and breathes
in the architecture of my womanhood.

This is a constellation drawn from the space between us,
and the gravity that kept pulling me home,
long after I had already gone.

Love in the Margins

She didn't speak love in the language I expected.
No lullabies, or declarations wrapped in ease.
But there were gestures - small acts of placement,
care arranged where no-one was looking.

She stitched tenderness into the edges of things
into meals and knitted corners of moments
folded tight against unravelling.

Her warmth lingered in arrivals,
in staying, in the silences
that settled instead of splintering.

I've come to learn that love doesn't always stand in the light.
Sometimes it waits in the margins
and yet leaves the page full.

My Mother's Daughter

I carry her in ways I cannot name:
In the way I answer the phone shoulders drawn,
a lighthouse bracing for a squall,
fixed and lit, unseen by those ashore.
Her love wasn't soft, but it was load-bearing.
It held like bedrock beneath shifting ground.
It holds me still: fierce, unshakable, true.

The Unfinished Script

It wasn't only love in her eyes
but something more angular:
expectation, the weight
of her own unfinished script
etched across the years.

When I succeeded, she hesitated
as if glimpsing a version of herself
she never reached,
a map she once drew
but never walked.

Still, there were moments in the hush before sleep
when her gaze softened,
like dusk settling softly over a worn verandah.

And in that quiet, I knew she had once dreamed
a gentler life for us both: one with fewer shadows,
more blue sky.

Uniform

She taught me to iron crease by crease
how order, disciplined and deliberate,
could hold chaos just beyond the frame.
Her uniform hung on the back of the door
a second skin pressed into precision,
stitched with resolve.
I memorised the lines
sharp, straight, unapologetic.

When I enter boardrooms,
silences and rooms full of men,
I recognise the straight lines
of coiled guardedness and pride
ironed into the very fibres of me.

Her Bruises Were Invisible

Her bruises were invisible, not the kind you see,
but the kind that throb when no one's looking.
She bruised in the muscles of silence
in the tight clasp of not asking for help.

The pain was never spoken.
But it rippled through the room when she left it.

And I, the daughter, became fluent in ache
without evidence.

Fierce

She entered a room the way flint meets stone
the quiet suggestion of spark.
Edges unsoftened, voice exact,
her truth folded inward,
not from fear, but deliberation.
A presence that struck against silence.

But I knew her softness - rare, unscheduled
in the way her fingers found my children's hair,
in the stillness she gave to a sunset,
as though colour might undo her.

She wasn't easy to hold but she held tight,
as one who had once been left behind
and vowed never to let go again.

She was not the fire. She was the flint
struck once, never forgotten.

And I carry her spark quietly, fiercely,
in the hollow of my hand.

Mirror

Sometimes, I glimpse her in my face
in the corners of my mouth when I am tired,
in the way I look away before I say what I mean.

I soften then.
Not for her.
But for me.

Because becoming her was never the fear,
only forgetting whom else I might be.

What I Would Say Now

You tried so hard to be steel
you forgot your body was water.
You cracked from trying not to bend.
And I, who learned from your silences
want to tell you: that I remember your laughter.
Even now, it's what I hear when I am brave.

Sunflowers

She loved sunflowers,
not roses, not lilies,
but the sun-drunk kind
that turned toward light
without apology.

There was something in them
that matched her spirit:
stubbornly facing forward.

She kept hand cream beside her bed,
rubbed it into her knuckles
as if softness could be coaxed
back into the places life had hardened.

With my children, she was gentler
offering biscuits and stories,
touching their faces as if she had been waiting
her whole life to be tender.

I saw her most clearly in those moments
when her edges blurred and her voice bent low,
a stem leaning just enough to meet the sun.

The Distance Between Us

We lived on different continents for most of my adult life.
Not estranged, just weathered by time zones,
by life seasons that refused to align.

Phone calls folded at the edges,
short, practical,
always slightly behind
what needed saying.

Still, she knew when my voice dipped,
when I paused too long between words.

And I knew
from the hush in her breathing,
the way she cleared her throat
before goodbyes that she loved me.
Fiercely.
Even if the words arrived late.

The map between us was wide
strung with the quiet certainty
that some threads hold
even across oceans.

The Season She Died

She died in winter,
when the mornings bruised blue
and the light arrived late.

The air in Africa felt unfamiliar without her breath in it
as if even the acacia knew something had shifted,
a root lifted, a sun withdrawn.

I flew home with grief packed poorly
creased into carry-on corners,
spilling at customs.

There was no house to return to, only the bones of one.
No place to lay her memory
that would not refuse to hold it long.

Even now, cold snaps remind me
of the deafening silence so complete
it made winter feel holy.

The House I Never Returned To

There's no home now, only coordinates
and a street that no longer knows my name.

She died, and the house folded in
a lung without its breath.
No scent in the drapes,
no ritual to anchor memory to a place.

But at four pm,
my phone still feels expectant.
I half-wait for the sunflower,
the single bloom she used to send me,
wordless, but saying everything.

I scroll through the silence,
as if love could still arrive
in a petal of code.

Some days that small icon feels more real
than the whole country I buried her in.

Everywhere and Nowhere

She is nowhere now, and everywhere:
In the pause before I speak,
in the spine of my daughter,
in the way certain silences feel inhabited.

I no longer beg time to return her.
Grief has softened into something quieter
a shadow I nod to, a weather I carry.

When four pm flickers and the sky turns slightly gold,
when a sunflower appears where it shouldn't,

I know she's not gone.
Just differently placed.

Fragments of her

My mother's voice lives in my bones,
a low drum under skin and sinew,
a tide of fire and whisper that rises
when the world bends too close.

Her scars are rivers beneath my flesh,
mapping paths I didn't choose but learned to walk –
each step a prayer, each breath a reckoning.

I gather fragments of her storms
and quiet moments,
forge them into armour
soft enough to feel, strong enough to carry forward

In this blood, I am both the wound and the healer
an unbroken thread woven through time.

Love at the Edges

Some forms of love do not arrive at the centre.
They gather at the thresholds in gestures half-completed,
in silences carried across continents,
in the space between what was offered and what was understood.

You learn to read absence like a second language,
to find meaning in the shape of the unsaid,
to carry warmth even when the room has gone cold.

Not all love is fluent. Not all love is whole.
Some of it still endures in the margins
soft-spoken, imperfect, and unforgotten.

Photo credit – Jade Holing Photography

NOTEBOOK THREE
LESSONS IN LIGHT AND LINE

24°59'45"S, 31°35'31"E

Field Note: Lessons in Light and Line

My father didn't pass down stories. He passed down attention, the angle of a glance, the pause between breath and speech, the way light stretches across a body when no one is watching. There's no vocabulary for what he gave. Only presence, a kind of quiet seeing shaped by place, somewhere just below the twenty-fifth line, where the veld casts long shadows and nothing speaks without meaning.

We didn't draw in those moments. That was never the purpose. What I learned wasn't art, but alignment. It wasn't about expression but a calibration: how to wait, how to witness without interrupting; how to hold the shape of something without needing to claim it.

Those early observations became a language: unspoken and spatial. It wasn't taught, it was absorbed. I didn't know then that I was learning restraint, that this was the beginning of line, not as mark, but as measure. He never called it teaching. But I carry it now in the way I frame a thought, in the distance I hold between knowing and naming, in the light I trace without needing to own. This is what line means to me: a boundary held with grace, a choice not to fill the silence, a way of showing what matters by what is left untouched.

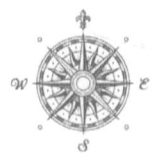

Lessons in Line

I learned to see before I found words
followed the curve of a heron's neck,
the shadow between antelope ribs,
the way light gathers in the curve of a horn.

My father taught presence as a kind of sight
the angle of elephant's shoulder,
the oxide hush of dust
after the first rain,
the discipline of returning
to the same stroke
until it speaks.

This is my apprenticeship
to line, to shadow,
to form, to the colour
humming ochre and restraint.

My thoughts carry the gifts of early still mornings,
wildlife stained with sun and attention,
of what it meant to study the world
until it revealed itself.

Some inherit power, others land.
I inherited patience and the unspoken covenant
between line and love.

The Language of Looking

Looking is not passive. It's a kind of speech
spoken through pigment and proximity.

The line is not a sentence. It is a decision.

I wrote a life in this kind of grammar
inexact, but articulate.

The Eye Before the Word

Before the sentence, there was the shape.
Contour, balance, shadow telling truth
in tones no tongue could name.

To draw is to dwell in the unspeakable
to name with line what language will only blur.

A Line that Believes

There's a kind of line that doesn't apologise,
one that knows its way around form
without insisting on mastery.

My father can draw with that kind of line.
He told me once,
"*You draw what you love by letting it breathe.*"

Colour

Cadmium red. Cobalt blue. Ochre, thick with memory.
He taught me the colours and the way they carry a history
you don't have to explain.
We didn't talk much about feelings
but he mixed them into every landscape.
And when I paint now, I speak in his colours.

Study of Light

He once said the hardest thing to paint was light:
not just how it falls, but what it reveals,
what it decides to love.
We sat for hours chasing the same shadow
as it moved across a jug of flowers
and the quiet weight of time.

Anatomy of Flight

I couldn't draw the lilac-breasted roller.
Not properly,
too much colour and too much wing.

"You're chasing the wrong thing," he said.
"Don't draw the feathers, draw the motion."

He sketched its shadow before its body.
And suddenly, I saw it.

The Weight of a Line

We draw the same impala:
his, fluid and sure;
mine, all bones and hope.

He doesn't correct me.
He draws beside me.
"The truest lines," he says,
*"are the ones you return to
again and again."*

Palette

He held the palette like a question
mixed colour to echo what light said about it.

Dust wasn't grey, it was burnt umber and skin.
The sky, more than blue
bone-white where it touched the trees.

I learned early: realism isn't repetition.
It's remembering what it felt like to look.

Earthy Tones

He painted in layers, acrylic drying too fast
unless you slowed your own hand.

The grass was never yellow:
it was nine kinds of ochre.
The shadows of a wildebeest
held violet and indigo, if you looked long enough.

Nothing in the wild is flat.
And nothing simple stays simple
once you've seen it properly.

Brushes

It's not music but it carries rhythm.
The swish of water,
the dry scratch of sable hair bristles
over an empty canvas.

He didn't need background noise.
The painting was its own voice.

I learned to listen in that hush.
And I still find a kind of home
in the silence that art makes possible.

Lineage

I am not a replica.
Lines of him streak through me:
his graphite on the grain of my paper.
He gave me his way of looking.
This way of being with nature, with people,
with what the world is always offering
if you're willing to see.

Negative Space

You taught me to leave some of the page untouched
out of reverence, not hesitation.

"White space is not emptiness",
you said. *"It's where the eye rests."*

Now, I carry that space into everything
a pause before reply, a hush before belief,
a quiet margin to frame what matters.

Underpainting

What they see is surface
the polished shape, the final hues
settled like dusk on a quiet plain.

But I remember the first layer- thin and wild,
sketched like wind across an open field
raw with intention.

I learned to paint from what isn't visible,
to build from undertones,
the earliest gesture buried
a load-bearing essence.

What's hidden doesn't vanish:
it echoes upward,
mapping longitude into every line
informing everything that follows.

His Hand Over Mine

Before I knew how light bends itself
to touch the rim of a cup,
he placed my hand in the hush
between gesture and grace.
No instructions,
just the stillness of a hawk
before descent, the silence where knowing begins.
He gave me the shape of attention.
A language of shadow and gleam.
And so I learned to look.
Not just at things, but into them
the way roots listen beneath the surface,
into the grain of things.

Acrylic

Acrylic dries quickly.
You must work fast,
decide before doubt has time
to enter the room.

No second-guessing. No going back.

My father liked it for this reason.
A truthfulness in the medium
that matched him.

I work slower.
But still, the quickening
lives in my hand.

Horizon Line

He taught me that the horizon bends.
The eye can't always be trusted.
The body remembers what the mind forgets.
The hand must follow the grain of feeling,
not the fiction of the line.
I still make that choice
in rooms that insist on angles
when I arrive as arc and drift.

Composition

"The eye needs balance," he said.
But balance isn't symmetry, it's weight placed with care.
So I set the shadows slightly off-centre,
left one corner bare.
And in that hush of space,
only the feeling
that something might arrive.

Fugitive

What endures is never the image
only the gaze that waits, unblinking.
Each line a threshold,
a pause before shape breathes into being.

Art taught me that love does not command,
it tunes. The hand doesn't guide
it listens for the fugitive pulse
beneath the visible.

To draw is to enter covenant
with what resists capture,
to honour the restless, the wild unspoken.
I come from that refusal,
and the quiet discipline
of staying just long enough
to know when to let go.

The line was never mine.
It moved through me a fugitive,
leaving in its wake
a shape I barely recognised as change.

Drawing Life

You begin with what you can hold:
a collarbone, light across the wrist.
Not the whole, just the gesture
an arc that suggests more than it shows.

To draw a life is not to mirror,
it's holding the pause
between breath and brush,
the place where bone
presses into memory.

Some lines must stay open.
They make space for silence to enter.

My father never said what mattered.
He showed me how long to wait
before the first mark
listening for the stillness beneath the eyes.

To draw a life is to love what slips your grip,
to remain with the trembling outline,
unwilling to force it closed.

NOTEBOOK FOUR
FAULT LINES

26°30'58"S, 29°12'10"E

Field Note on Drift

There was a time I mistook stillness for certainty. The days followed one another in practised order, each gesture a thread in a life I believed I was still weaving. The weight was familiar, the walls, intact. I held the shape of the life we had built, even as it began to change around me.

But stone remembers the river, even after the current has moved on. The pattern loosened slowly. The rooms were filled with the same light, but it no longer touched me the same way. I moved through the days like a figure traced in chalk, present, but no longer anchored. A quiet unravelling had begun, though I could not yet name it.

There was no rupture, only the ache of absence taking root. A life can hollow without breaking. A vow can remain spoken, even as it no longer shelters. I had not imagined leaving. I had imagined staying. But imagination, it turns out, is no match for drift.

This is what remains: the knowledge that something can be real and still be lost, that a life can dissolve around you while you hold it with both hands. I stepped away only when the ground had altered so completely that it no longer recognised the weight of my staying.

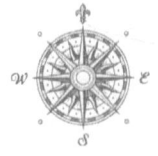

Tectonics

Some fractures begin in the marrow
where weight compacts over time,
where habit ossifies into form,
and breath must carry
what bone cannot voice.

The map lives in the places
where structure falters
and the self stretches
to accommodate what no longer fits.

It is a cartography of dissonance:
migrations of belief,
the tectonic drift of love,
the strange fidelity to a name
that no longer contains your becoming.

Fault lines are records of motion.
Proof that something moved
with magnitude, and left the shape of its passing.

Fracture

It didn't break. It slipped quietly:
a shoreline yielding in plain sight.
In the morning, the door resisted its frame,
the house sighed and the birds went quiet.

I knew in my blood
that something once whole
had frayed to a thread then vanished.
The fracture was not the end.
It was recognition of a line traced inward
to where ancient knowing
had waited all along.

Artefact

At the back of a drawer I found it:
a scarf I once wore
through a season that nearly broke me.

It still held the scent of wind,
dry leaves and an argument I never finished.

I didn't cry. Just held it like a relic
soft, creased at the corners,
no longer meant to warm, but to remind.

Not everything that survives is whole.
Some things stay only so we can see
how far we've come.

Kin and Ash

Betrayal by blood reorients the map
veins reroute, marrow recoils,
and the body no longer believes its own design.

It doesn't tear, it unravels,
shatters the seam where loyalty
was assumed sacred.

It burns inward, splintering bone from marrow,
unmaking what was meant to hold.

What breaks is not love,
rather the covenant beneath it
a sacred oath written in blood,
that kin would never be the hand
to shatter the sacrament of trust
bound by name, by lineage, by bone.
And still, you carry it the name,
the silence, the scar.
Kin and ash. Both inherited.
Both irreversible.

Pilcrow

It came mid-sentence, a hook of breath,
inked pause, a pivot in the margin of my life.

I marked the page, the breath-held hinge
where the story turned and I stood,
voice feathered with flint, lifting from marrow into air.

This was a reckoning etched in the marrow,
a fault line, long quiet, beginning to hum.
The insult didn't wound, it summoned.

Dignity broke her silence - a lioness rising,
determination honed by generations,
eyes steady on the breach.

Each breath held the weight of women
who walked edges no map could name,
and crossed ruin without fracture.
I didn't speak. I stood
and every bone bore witness.

What I Keep Now

I no longer keep the sharp answers,
the rehearsed explanations,
the need to be understood on the first try.

Now, I keep a soft coat by the door,
a handful of names that still feel like home,
and the discipline of walking away without bitterness.

Because the Moon is Still Here

The news is loud again. People say the world is slipping.
And yet the kettle still hums. The dogs still dream.
The moon still holds its soft, disinterested light over all of us.

Not indifference. Just permanence.
The kind that reminds me
that some things were built to endure
whether or not we understand them.

Elegy for the Unlived Life

Some doors I never walked through.
Some names I never became.

They live quietly in the background,
rooms where I once imagined myself unfolding.
I light a candle for those ghosts,
a gentle flame to whisper:
I saw you, too.

The Use of Small Things

A teaspoon. A folded cloth.
Fresh apples in a bowl.
The silence in the room after the kettle clicks.
Some days meant for quiet completion.
For gratitude and being kind
to what is already here.

What the Wind Remembers

The wind remembers the sigh my body gave
as it released its grip,
the hush of my stillness
when the last leaf of care
slipped softly, without protest.

Between the Lines

Some knowing doesn't fade, it shifts.
I still read your grammar:
the way your jaw tightens before a storm,
the pause just before you speak
and the shape
of what you choose to leave behind.

Whatever else was lost, this remains:
a map I still carry of how you move
beneath your own silence.

The Body Remembers

My body gathers ache like rainwater,
holds the rhythm of tides beneath skin,
recalls the reach of branches
stretching toward sun,
the wild generosity of lungs
opening again and again,
insisting on life
long after the storms have passed.

Unfinished Things

Once, I hurried to close loops,
tie bows, stamp sentences shut.
Now I leave poems open,
their endings unfastened,
lines still breathing,
long after I've walked away.

Some Days Are Wide

Some days feel like open windows
the kind you don't remember opening
but suddenly, there's breeze
birdsong and a bowl of pears lit just right.

Nothing is solved.
But for a moment, the world agrees with itself
and I am allowed to rest inside it.

Solitude

There is a silence that builds itself
not so much absence, but a kind of structure.
Bone-white scaffolding where touch once lived,
every beam strained with what might return.

In the late light, I fold the day into corners:
a teaspoon resting on the counter,
steam rising from a cup meant for two,
a coat still hanging, still hoping.

Longing isn't a storm, it's the still water
that doesn't ripple, doesn't dry.
It's the way a shadow leans toward
the sound of your name, even when unsaid.

I've learned the shape of solitude:
not sharp, not bitter,
but vast, a cathedral carved from the ache of waiting.

I light the lamp, open the window,
somewhere out there, the world aches back.

A Practice of Staying

The temptation is always to go
to change your name,
your hair, your horizon,
your weather.

But I have learned to stay,
to greet the same windows
each morning with different eyes.
To hold my restlessness
like a seed of potential
that hasn't cracked yet.

NOTEBOOK FIVE
MILK AND MEASURE

33°52′4″S, 151°12′26″E

Field Note on Children

They began inside me, but that was only the first chapter. The deeper becoming came later, when their bodies no longer pressed against mine, but their needs threaded through every hour. Their names redefined urgency, recalibrated my thresholds for fear and wonder, rewrote the logic of sleep and silence.

Motherhood never announced itself as a role. It revealed itself as a landscape, crossed barefoot and unprepared. Some days were lush with joy, others flinted with resistance. I built direction from repetition, learned to interpret fever and frown, distinguished one silence from another. Love was never abstract. It lived in muscle, in reflex, in the vigilance that becomes second nature.

Now they live beyond the reach of my hands. They carry their own keys, speak languages I did not teach them, stake claims in worlds I can't fully enter. And still, I feel their weather. Joy rises in my chest before the message arrives. I find myself setting places for them in thought, unconsciously.

I do not long for who they were. I stand in awe of who they are becoming. And yet, beneath my ribs, I still carry the imprint of their breath, small, steady, formative. It remains a rhythm within me. A quiet governance I never chose to relinquish.

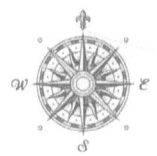

Milk

I measured love in ounces,
in the weight of sleep surrendered,
in the way my name changed
in the mouths of my children.

There are no blueprints for how to hold a life.
Only instinct. And the slow acquisition of attention.

I mothered without manuals
measuring fever with the back of my hand,
learning when to loosen the grip
so they could grow toward their own shape.

This is a quiet apprenticeship:
to sleepless devotion,
to the language beneath their language,
to the weight of knowing
they would leave me
if I had done it right.

Milk was only the beginning.
The real nourishment was made
in the hours no one witnessed
in the calibration of love to need,
presence to absence, closeness to letting go.

There are hopes I whispered
into rooms where they had already gone.
The rituals. The relenting.
The fierce, exacting art of staying
close while stepping back.

The Shape of Their Names

-26.5097° latitude, 29.2022° longitude

Before I knew them,
I tried on names like dresses
holding each one to the light,
wondering who they'd become.
But the truth is, their names fit them
long before I spoke them.
Some names you give.
Some names teach you who you are.

The Light She Keeps

(For my daughter)

You made the world louder
vibrant with colour
in the way you named things,
bold and out of order,
as if rules were suggestions
not quite worthy of you.

I watched you become a flare.
More than a flower,
a wild seed flung free
dancing where the wind is curious.

And still when you rest your head
against my shoulder,
I am the place your fire forgets
it ever needed a match.

Quiet Intelligence

(For my son)

You entered the world
with eyes that felt older than mine,
serious, searching,
already full of questions
that reached beyond your years,
asked not to impress,
but to understand.

With you, joy arrived in sudden belly-laughs,
the quiet wonder of impossible questions,
in bedtime spirals of thought
that folded into dreams
neither of us could quite explain.

I loved your softness most
not because it needed shielding,
but because it held its own quiet force.
Even now, your silence steadies me
as presence in its most deliberate form.

Just Enough

(For my son)

You came in barefoot, dust tracing the hem of your silence,
sun caught in your hair and sat with me in my heartache
for a few moments. No questions. Only knowing.
Your hand, brief against mine,
then the soft exit, bare feet returning to the day outside.

I smiled, because you knew and didn't name it.
Because you left just enough love
to brighten my day.

The Watch

(For my daughter)

You've never needed warning.
You read the air the way some read a room
quick, ready to step between
what might bruise and what matters to you.

I am not fragile, but you guard me
as if you've decided that strength runs both ways
and love means taking the first blow,
even when it never comes.

There is fire in you, but it is controlled.
A perimeter, not a blaze.

I've learned not to argue with your instincts.
You are your own compass.
And I, unexpectedly, have become a place
you fiercely defend.

Calibration

-25.8381° latitude, 28.2226° longitude

I knew how much to say
and when to hold silence
not to protect you from truth,
but to give you room to grow
into your own questions.

In the Small Hours

It wasn't the birthdays or the framed things.
It was how you leaned into me
in checkout queues, mud on your cuffs,
one sock half-slid down your heel,
your trust as casual as breath.

It was cereal at odd hours,
questions with no answers,
the way your feet swung
beneath the table like clocks not yet set
to the speed of the world.

We laughed over burnt toast,
soggy school notes, and a dog that barked at clouds.

That was the joy:
not the milestones, the middle.
the moments the music made
of days we didn't know we'd miss.

All the Ways I Stayed

Not all staying looks like standing still.
Some days, it was holding the thread
with teeth, while my hands did something else.

It was being the shadow in your doorway,
the breath behind your name,
the soft boundary that let you fall
without breaking.

You may never see all the ways I stayed.
But you walk on the floorboards
I nailed down in prayers while you slept.

The Leaving Begins Early

-33.7225° latitude, 151.0427° longitude

It starts long before the suitcase
in the way they stop calling your name
from the hallway,
the way their arms find other anchors.

You notice it in the shoes by the door
that no longer belong to childhood,
in the silence that grows
between dinner and bedtime.

They leave in increments, slipping through gaps
you didn't know were openings.

And you smile, you nod, you hand them the keys.

But later, in the stillness, you place your hand
over the hollow and you name it grace.

Chapters

They carried off whole chapters
I didn't know were mine:
my laugh, my sleep,
the way I once walked
without checking the clock.

They wore my shirts to paint in,
used my words to argue with their teachers,
left fingerprints on the mirror
of who I thought I'd be.

And still, I'd give them more
from the kind of love
that doesn't count the cost
until silence falls.

Even then, it felt like winning.
Even now, I would give it again.

Vow at Latitude Twenty South

-20.2826° latitude, 149.0380° longitude

She stood barefoot at the edge of the world
the sea holding its breath,
the air thick with salt and blessing.

I watched her cross an invisible line
not marked in sand,
but drawn somewhere just beneath the ribs.

Her laughter, half wind, half vow,
rose like a flare into the light.
And I knew: my girl was gone.
The woman was choosing
a new kind of belonging.

They faced each other
beneath a sky I could not frame,
light split open like the hush before rain.

Later, I pressed the warmth of the day into memory.
A quiet latitude, twenty degrees south,
where my heart squeezed
and let her go, without breaking.

Quiet Strength

He doesn't flinch at her storm-weather moods
just waits, steady as a hillside,
until the winds quiet.

His strength is in the daily rituals:
knowing when to speak and when to listen,
when to stand beside her, and when to step back
so she can rise without resistance.

I've watched him tend love like a field
with patience, with care, and the quiet dignity
of someone who never needed to prove
what was already rooted.

I've seen him tend to her joy
and her quiet with equal reverence.

This is the kind of man who does not mark his presence,
he marks his word.

Latent Geometry

(for my son)

You work in precision,
numbers arranged like scaffolding,
risk calculated down to its smallest margin,
outcomes projected, held to account.

Still, your hands recall something older:
the rhythm of the wheel,
the way wet clay listens when held just right,
how form rises from touch more than command.

You move between frameworks
formulas that demand certainty,
and vessels that bloom from uncertainty.
Both require your full attention.
Both reveal their fault lines
when handled without care.

I watch you solve for structure by day,
then return to the kiln
the fire reflecting in your face,
as if some part of you answers to heat,
to patience, to the slow transformation of earth
into something that holds.

You have become a man of both disciplines,
one who knows that accuracy can serve beauty,
and that tenderness can live
in even the most exacting design.

You hold what is measurable
alongside what resists measure,
and you do not flinch.

You remain present to both
your hands steady, your center intact.

The One Who Loves Him

She loved him without blueprint or claim
not for what he could become,
but for the shape he already held.

She understood the quiet architecture of presence
how to stay near without encircling,
how to listen without needing reply.

He never noticed the shift at first
how she left room for him to be whole
without being fixed.

She didn't trace his edges to contain him,
only to see where the light might best fall.

And maybe that was the art of it
not the love that asked for more,
but the one that made space for all he was.

Proposal at Forty-One North

41.4145° latitude, 2.1527° longitude

Parc Güell, Barcelona

You asked for my blessing,
and something in me,
equal parts wonder and memory, unlocked.
You needed no permission,
but you knew what it meant to ask.

In that garden of fractured light
and rising colour, you knelt on mosaic stone,
Gaudí beneath you, future before you
and offered your yes to her.

I wasn't there. But I see it clearly:
the curve of her mouth just before she said it,
the tremble in your hand
as everything aligned
intention, devotion, sky.

You chose a place built on art and vision
where structure curves and beauty resists symmetry.
Fitting, I think, for the beginning of something true.

And I, I gave you my blessing without hesitation.
Not as ritual, but as recognition:
you had grown into the kind of man
who asks with grace and means it.

Latitude Twenty-Seven South

-27.4679° latitude, 153.0281° longitude

She lives where the river curves like a question,
where storms arrive sudden and full of intention.
I learn her weather from the pauses in our calls,
from the arc of her voice when she says she's fine.

There is no sadness in this, only the slight ache
of a season changing
before you've put away your coat.

She carries pieces of me,
both inheritance and instinct:
the way she pauses before speaking,
how she reads a room without apology.

And I, I walk each morning under a different sky,
grateful for the latitude that let us both grow wide.

Widening

They are no longer small enough to gather with a glance.
I watch them now like weather
not to predict, but to witness what arrives.

Their lives spool outward, thread by thread,
in colours I did not choose but recognise in my bones.
This is not the part I was warned about
the gentle ache of irrelevance,
the beauty of being unnecessary.

And still, I hold the shape
of having loved them completely.
A widening kind of grace
that does not cling.

We Grew Up Together

They say I raised you, but some days,
it felt like you held the compass.
You steadied the storm in me
with the quiet gravity
of small hands reaching.

You taught me patience without words,
in the long pause and held breaths
before a tantrum passed,
in shoelaces knotted by sheer will.
We mapped love without instructions
a path forged in blanket forts,
spilled cereal, morning coffee
and late-night questions
I didn't always answer right.

In your eyes I caught my reflection
exhausted, but still seen – a face softened by trying.
We were all new to this.
Yet, look at the distance we've crossed
with laughter threaded through the cracks
of every day.

Their Laughter, My Home

No architect could have drawn
a sound more perfect than their laughter
bouncing down the hallway,
spilling through the kitchen,
cracking like light beneath the door.

I have lived in many places
rented, bought, built, rebuilt
but none more solid
than the moment both their voices rose at once,
fighting and forgiving in the same breath.

If you ask me what I'll remember,
it won't be the grades, the beds I made,
or the rules we enforced
and forgot.

It will be the laughter.
And how I knew without needing to look
that I belonged there.

A Quiet Kind of Pride

I watch the way they move through the world
gentle with strangers, fierce with injustice,
kind to animals and uncertain people.

That is enough. More than enough.
To know they are good where it really matters.

A Kind of Forever

I always knew they wouldn't stay
not in this house, not in the hush
of story time and scattered blocks.

But they rewired my seeing.
Milk in the fridge means more now: ritual, return.
Sunday still carries the shape of their voices,
how they once named it ours.

Wherever they go,
my life keeps time with theirs
the angles of worry,
the radiance of becoming,
the imprint of love
in corners no one else would think to look.

This unshakeable quiet is its own kind of forever.

Thread

Even now, I feel the thread
not tugging, just there,
a tension that hums quietly
beneath the day.

They don't need me to hold them anymore,
but something in me still wraps their names
around morning light,
around the echo of doors closing.

Motherhood doesn't end.
It just changes its grammar from doing to being,
from presence to knowing.

Letter for Later

I don't expect you to understand now.
Now is for your speed, your noise,
your beautiful forgetting.

But one day when you sit in the stillness
of your own becoming,
when something you love breaks
and you keep going
you might remember the way I stayed.
Not just in rooms, but in presence.
Not just with meals, but with love.
And I hope it finds you not as guilt, but as grace.
Not as a weight, but as a way.

Interlude

There are roles we step into
before we've fully arrived.

Motherhood taught me how to stretch,
not just time, but self.

How to love in layers:
with urgency, with restraint,
with the grace to become invisible
just long enough for them to shine.

It is about becoming.
It is about carrying life and learning
when to set it down.

Milk and Memory

She fed them from a body she no longer owned.
Each cry a small earthquake.
Each dawn a baptism in fatigue.

But now, years later
she watches their backs cross a parking lot
and feels the ache of what was hers
and no longer needs to be.

NOTEBOOK SIX
SALT AND BONE

33°43'45"S, 151°0'14"E

Field Note on What Remains

After the breaking, you brace for absence. But what startled me most was presence in the way memory clings, quiet and insistent, to objects, to the corners of rooms, to the cadence of breath. Grief doesn't dissolve; it settles into longitude and the fall of light, into the fault lines of the body. It becomes an internal weather system, shifting but always there.

Not everything can be retrieved. But some things, the elemental ones, refuse to leave. They root beneath language. They embed in marrow. They become map. You learn to live by coordinates no-one else can see, but that orient you all the same. A private cartography. A precise, unspoken bearing.

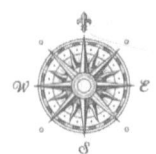

Elemental

Some breaks are quiet.
Elemental, a dissolution so intimate
you feel it in the marrow
before the mind can name it.

This is not an inventory of blame.
It is a record of aftermath:
the grief that calcifies,
the tenderness that lingers
long after the door has closed.

Love does not disappear.
It distills into rituals of restraint,
into the long ache of memory
carried in the bones
long after it ceases to speak.

What remains is not ruin. It is residue.
Salt on skin, a structure uninhabited
but still intact.

Salt and Bone

You loved me with a hunger
that sounded like prayer
and moved like possession.

I mistook your wanting for wonder,
let it hollow me until even silence
echoed your name.

You didn't leave gently. You receded,
as water pulling back from a ruined shore.
What remained was wreckage:
splinters, salt in the shape of memory,
bone where a body had hoped.

There was no soft ending,
no folded note. But in your absence,
I learned the tensile strength of skin,
the echo of touch
that becomes its own anthem.

I am not unmade, only returned,
to the salt, to the bone,
to what endures after the wave.

Seahorse

You placed it in my palm
small as a breath held too long,
a fossilised seahorse,
curled in on itself like a secret.

Stone-boned and ancient,
its spine a fine thread of memory,
looped into permanence.

You said it once lived where oceans now forget.
And I, still learning the weight
of delicate things, understood only this:
it had endured by becoming something else.

I kept it beside brushes and pigment,
a creature stilled but not silenced.
Its hush taught me that wonder can harden
without losing grace,
that even the smallest things can outlast the tide.

And in that gift, quiet, unwrapped,
you gave me more than artefact.
You gave me the shape of resilience.

When it Broke

-33.7324° latitude, 151.0074° longitude

She didn't move at first.
Her body hadn't caught up
with what the house already knew.
The door was still ajar, tea cooling in his cup.
She walked barefoot to the spot where his voice
still hung in the air,
touched the chair he'd leant on for a hint of warmth.
She didn't cry that night.
She just swept the pieces into her own hands,
and held them until they stopped trembling.

The Exit

I thought love had a louder exit.
But you slipped between Tuesdays,
unhooking your name from the rhythm of the day.

I kept the shape of you like a bruise remembers impact
a shadow that darkened before it lightened.

The house did not fall, but something foundational tilted.

And I, setting the table,
kept calling your name
into the echo, just to prove
you'd once belonged there.

What Love Did

It didn't break me - It rearranged me
moved the windows,
sanded the floorboards,
repainted the walls in colours I didn't choose.

I came out redrawn, stitched with new margins,
carrying the architecture of having once been opened.

Remains

There are rooms in me you never fully left.
The air remembers your voice,
even if I do not call it.
The doorframe still leans
as if expecting your shadow.

You are not here,
but the walls carry your echo
like a scent that won't wash out.

I rearranged the furniture.
I painted over the cracks.
Still, beneath the surface,
you remain in quiet architecture
of what was once almost home.

Sediment

Grief settles behind the sternum low and tidal,
silt in the bend of a river long after the flood has passed.

Some mornings, it wakes before I do
a pressure in the lungs,
a heaviness braided into the ache behind the eyes.

I carry it the way cliffs hold weather without protest,
just the slow darkening of weathered stone.

It moves through me - a second skin
creased in the joints, lined with salt,
warmed by the body that still refuses to break.

Grief is not a burden anymore.
It is a rhythm - a tide I know how to stand in
without drowning.

Antithetical

She grows not like ivy, creeping, clinging
but like stone warming in sunlight.
She speaks less but says more.
And the room adjusts around her
instead of the other way.

Portrait in Late Light

She does not look like she used to.
There is something looser in the way she smiles,
less curated, more elemental.

She is not soft because she's been spared.
She is soft because she's endured
without becoming stone.

Brink

I learned to live with it,
like an old seam in the earth
that keeps quiet until it doesn't.

There were years we stood on the same side of silence.
I still remember your first laugh in my kitchen,
the way love found a language
before we found the words.

I won't call it a wound.
It's geography now mapped by memory,
not regret.

Some things break without breaking us.

Another Way to Know

I used to ask for signs.
Now I look at the shape of the morning light
on the dogs' backs. I don't need proof.
Only pattern. Only presence.
Only this.

After

There is a kind of beauty in the remains
not the burn,
but what stays after flame.

I didn't choose the ending, but I stood in it,
barefoot, not asking for rescue.

You learn, in the hush after leaving,
that some love lingers
not to haunt, but to remind.

Even salt is what keeps the water from rotting.

Cairn

What once lived at the axis of my breath settled,
not undone, but reformed into weight.
I did not grieve in the language of endings.
I built a cairn stone by stone,
each one a fragment of what held,
what fractured, what still speaks
when the wind changes direction.

Some mornings I pass the place
where we came apart and feel the pull,
faint as a compass buried beneath frost.

The structure remains:
lopsided, weathered, but utterly mine.
A geometry of what endured.
Memory with mass.
Love, refigured in the language of stone.

Remains

There are endings that leave no debris,
only altered ground.

You learn to walk differently
because the terrain no longer responds
in quite the same way.

There is no monument. No wound to dress.
Only a shift in the body's compass,
a tenderness where certainty once stood.

Yet, in the absence of return, you know it mattered
because it moved something elemental in you.

And movement, however quiet, leaves its mark.

To Stay Human

I watered the plant too much again.
Still, it reaches for the window
like forgiveness was written into its roots.

The dogs knocked over my coffee
not to spite me, but because their world
is made of movement curiosity and soft chaos.

The wind slammed the door. I did not scold it.
I've come to accept that even the house has its moods.

So much is outside of us.
So much depends on not hardening
when things go wrong.

To stay human, I've learned,
is not to stay whole,
but to breathe through the cracks,
to speak gently when you could be right,
to reach across the silence
instead of filling it.

Kindness isn't weakness.
It's what keeps the thread unbroken.
Even now. Especially now.

Reconstruction

Hope doesn't return whole.
It comes in pieces - a hand offered
a letter kept, a crack of blue at the edge of storm.

You don't trust it at first. You test the weight,
wait for the collapse.
But it stays. And then, so do you.

You lift the beam. You patch the roof.
You build again, because something in you
refuses to leave the foundation empty.

Hope

Hope doesn't wait. It pushes through ash,
through ice-thick soil, through the wreckage
you thought was final.

It is the muscle that mends in silence,
the nerve that fires after the break.
Hope is what insists on morning,
even when the sky stays dark.

It isn't gentle. It doesn't ask.
It moves in you, grit in the blood,
a forward-making force you didn't summon
but cannot stop.

Dandelion Woman

She grows where concrete forgets how to soften.
In the quiet margin, she lifts her face to light
bright, untamed, wholly her own.

Wind does not startle her.
She leans, bends, holds,
roots deep in unsung places,
grace threaded through grit.

Some call her wild. Some try to name her ruin.
Still, she opens: petals gold with memory,
a lineage of endurance unwritten in books.

Children see her clearly: a wish cradled in their breath,
a soft thing strong enough to travel far.

She blooms even when no one asked her to.
Her roots remember what the world forgets:
how to hold fast, how to let go, how to shine.

NOTEBOOK SEVEN
FLINT

33°50'19"S, 151°12'2"E

Field Note on Flint

Flint does not announce itself through beauty. It was never meant for display. It lies buried in ancient layers, dense and exact, waiting for the hand that knows how to read its grain.

In the old world, it became edge, shaped into an arrowhead, blade, fire-starter. Every fracture deliberate. Every angle drawn with consequence. Flint gave direction to force. It made survival possible. It turned pressure into purpose.

There is a lineage in that. A way of being in the world that does not waver or decorate, but sharpens inward, choosing clarity over excess. Flint holds its shape under contact. It leaves a mark because it was designed to.

This notebook is for the women who have been pressed into the syntax of others, taught to pare themselves down to fit. But flint is not meant to bend. It cleaves when it must: flesh from bone, truth from pretence. Yet it also carries spark, the capacity to ignite, to catch, to light what must finally burn. What follows is shaped from that fire. Boundary is its architecture. Impact, its language. What endures is the woman who holds her edge and chooses when to strike.

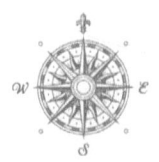

Flint

She never sought the fire.
But life struck bone against bone,
flint sparked in the marrow
answer dark with ember.
Call it stubbornness. Call it faith.
Call it the quiet violence
of surviving with grace.

Spine

I learned to steady my voice when others rose,
to measure each word like salt in bread,
to stay present without needing to be seen.

Some forms of strength are lived,
carried in the body, held in the pause before reaction.

Stillness has structure.
And mine is made of the times I stayed
not from silence, but from conviction.

There is power in speaking without urgency,
in knowing what matters enough to answer
and what doesn't.

Dominion

I move differently now: not lighter, but attuned.
I no longer yield to rooms that shrink me,
or shrink myself to hold the peace.

What they mistook for softness was calculation:
the long art of staying silent until the shape of truth could hold.

I rebuilt slowly from blueprint from the aching geometry
of who I was before I bent.

Now, I carry no permission slips.
My footsteps are fluent in thresholds.
I do not wait to be seen.

This is not a return: it is dominion,
the sovereign act of inhabiting my own name.

Theory of Quiet Things

Some truths are too tender for language.
They live in the boiled egg, peeled slowly,
thumb sliding under the shell
as if not to startle the morning.
In the dog's sigh beneath the table,
in the way she lets someone finish
though she already holds the ending
cupped gently, like water in her hands.

They reside in the pause before correction,
in the soft closing of cupboards,
in knowing when to stay
and when to leave the light on.

These are not the loud truths,
the ones that insist.
They are the undercurrent
that steadies the whole house.

Proof, With Paws

They don't speak, but they know.
How to wait without question,
how to follow without fear.
The black one moves like a thought
half-held, close, observant,
carrying stillness as knowing.
The caramel one moves like a flame
quick to joy, certain of welcome,
never needing permission to belong.
They mark the hours by footsteps,
the seasons by tone.
Some days, they are the only
proof I need that love can be
instinctive, and soft things can last.

What To Do With Fire

I carry flame in a lantern of my own making,
trim the wick, shield the light,
feed it through hours that ask for more than heat.

I don't burn bridges. I walk back across them,
hands cupped around the glow,
warming myself with what I chose to keep alive.

I stay after the noise recedes, gather what was overlooked,
write in the margins where meaning tends to hide.

This is not ambition. It is ember kept alive,
a quiet heat that refuses to surrender.

No Urgency

I do not rush to catch what falls.
Not every fracture requires my hands.

Some truths need the slow kiln of silence to harden.
Some answers arrive better unhurried.

I let questions echo now
let them stretch their limbs in the dark
without chasing them down.

Even stillness can speak when given the time.

In Praise of Enough

The pot didn't boil over.
The email was kind.
My breath held steady in the cold.

No one asked for more than I had.
No part of me demanded
what I couldn't give.

Today, I did not reach for better.
I simply said: *this is enough,* and meant it.

When It is Quiet

The hum in my chest isn't fear anymore.
It's a vital current - raw, steady,
a wind threading through wire
light waking the edges of stone.
It was always there.
I don't flee the silence anymore.
I listen. Let it rise around me
like a clearing after rain,
sharp with scent and full of space.

And somewhere beneath the stillness,
beneath breath and bone,
a voice I almost forgot
says clearly: *You survived.*

What Isn't Said

She writes letters she doesn't send,
tells stories that end in silence.

Not everything needs to be spoken.
Some truths live best in the space
between breath and word.

Shear Line: A Theory of Stress

There is a place where forces converge
opposing, unyielding
and the body learns how to carry both.

A seam runs through me,
quiet as a blueprint,
marking where weight settles,
where tension recalculates
its path through flesh and will.

Stress has direction. It moves inward,
settles behind the ribs,
compresses thought into action,
hours into angles.

I track the strain,
load shifting from shoulder to spine,
tendons tightening into lines that hold.

The body becomes a kind of scaffolding
temporary in surface, enduring beneath.
Every movement a measured transfer,
each breath a small recalibration.

Stillness does not enter.
The work is constant, redistribution,
containment, resistance made elegant
by necessity.

Relief arrives through expansion,
through the widening of internal space
where force once pressed.

I remain intact configured for impact.
This is the mark of bearing well:

the line that runs through me
without tearing.

Voice

I didn't lose it, I lent it to polished rooms
and suited certainty,
to men who mistook silence
for absence, and conviction
for compliance.

I let my voice fill the spaces they stood in,
sanded down my edges so their echoes
could sound uninterrupted.

My voice gathers now at the back of my throat,
a tide remembering the shore,
it returns with marrow, salt and staying power.
And this time, I speak only where I mean to.

Assumptions

They thought I bent.
They mistook flexibility for fragility.
But the spine knows its strength
in remembering how to rise.

The Law of Conservation

Nothing is lost they say, only changed.
Energy becomes heat. Love becomes memory.
A voice becomes the echo you follow inward.

What he took did not vanish.
It rearranged into silence I now inhabit
like a language I once knew.

Somewhere, in the algebra of aftermath,
my name resolves not as what was left,
but what remained.

I am not what broke. I am what endured
under the pressure of revision.

Letter to the Self That Waited

You were never naïve
to stand with the door unlatched.
Hope was not frailty, it was fortitude
in its most tender form.

But let me say this: the life you inhabit
is no consolation prize.
It is not the residue of what was refused.

It is breath that answers only to you,
a dwelling shaped in slow devotion,
fitted to the architecture of your becoming.

Each wall bears your name in its grain.
Even the silence echoes in your voice.

Holding the Line

I leave no signature, only pressure points,
the grain shifted by a hand that held steady
when no one watched.

You won't see my name etched into the finish,
but the shape holds because I was there,
bearing weight where it would have given.

That is the mark. That is the proof.

Learning Stillness

Not the kind practiced on polished floors
spine aligned, palms lifted
as if waiting for permission.
But the stillness that arrives unbidden,
when the clatter has emptied itself,
and the body recalls
it no longer needs to brace.
Only breath remains
anchored, unchoreographed.
And above, a sky wide enough
to hold you without question.

Kindness Misread

They called it soft,
my open hand, my willingness to explain.
They did not know I had learned to wield empathy
as a blade pressed flat.
It never breaks skin, but it cuts just the same.

When the Blade Turns

There comes a moment
when I no longer soften the blow
when the breath I once offered
becomes steel drawn clean.

I stop translating myself for comfort.
Let silence fill what others failed to ask.

The edge that once lay hidden beneath grace
gleams now without apology.
This is the mercy of no longer bleeding
to keep the peace.

What They Don't See

They see composure - a voice smooth as glass.
They don't see the grip beneath the table,
breath counted like coins,
the quiet geometry of holding it all together.

They don't smell the smoke,
don't notice the burn threaded into my sleeves.
They don't know how many fires I put out
with my hands still burning.

She Left Without Leaving

There are ways a woman goes without taking a step.
She unthreads herself from the centre outward
a voice dimmed to avoid echo,
a presence reduced to function and form.
Her answers become efficient.
Her laughter, archived.

No-one notices the outline softening,
the slow retreat behind her eyes.
She wasn't valued, so she stopped answering.
Some departures leave everything
in its place, except the woman.

Shape of Her Name

They tried to name her with one word.
But she kept growing out of it,
changing edges, building light in places
no one had mapped.

She is more than daughter.
More than lover. More than vessel.
She is the fire and the clay.
The water and the pot it fills.
Call her nothing she has not chosen.

Rite

She coaxes flame from the stove's cold mouth,
tending heat as if summoning presence.
The cloth moves across the counter
to consecrate, each pass an inscription
in the grain of things that hold.

Nothing in this room is idle.
The kettle breathes. The walls remember.
Even the silence knows its part.

This is not routine. It is rite.
A way to say: I am still here, intact,
in offering, worthy of warmth.

Threshold

Somewhere between who she was
and who she is becoming
there is a room with no door.

Only breath. Only a chair.
Only enough stillness to listen
to the part of her that has waited for years
to be heard.

At the Edge of the Day

There is a moment just before evening
when the house exhales
the kettle cooling, dogs curled,
the windows streaked with gold.

And I am reminded
that peace is not a place I find
but something that finds me
when I stop searching.

Keys

You kept the porch light burning long after the night lost interest,
swept the threshold clean, polished the handles
as if readiness alone could summon a guest.

You mistook the stillness for waiting,
the silence for absence, not knowing it was you
tracing the shape of your own return.

The keys were never lost.
They lived in the lining of your coat,
stitched into the seams of your undoing,
warmed by the body that bore them.

Now when you cross the threshold,
doors open at your touch,
air holds your shape,
and every room remembers.
You were always the one who held the keys.

Script

I was not drafted in haste.
Each stroke required intention,
ink drawn slow from reservoir to rag paper,
the page absorbing what I could not name aloud.

No-one else held the nib.
Even when the line faltered,
I followed through the pressure stroke,
let the flaw become part of the form.

Some ascenders leaned too far,
some counters remained open.
Margins shifted, guidelines blurred.
still I returned, each gesture a reclamation.

Some days I traced only the baseline.
Others, a ligature emerged,
linking one quiet truth to the next.

This was never imitation.
Every loop, every serif,
every breath between glyphs, mine.

Not perfect. Not planned.
But ink that will not lift from the page.

Heretic

I torched the pages,
unleashing words that bound me,
releasing ink-stained phantoms
of stories carved by others' hands.

Flames hungrily devoured the edges,
crackling like prayers torn open,
smoke curling thick, suffocating confessions
of half-truths I refuse to carry.
Their doctrine, bloodied by Fear,
whispered by Doubt turned to ash.

I become the heretic,
exiled from the library of expectation,
scrawling in the embers
a savage new language of freedom:
where every spark ignites a seed,
and every burn scorches a beginning.

Bless the Unfinished

Bless the poems that falter mid-line,
where meaning gathers in the slow light of dawn.

The beds left tangled,
linen folds clutching stories of nights unquiet,
and grief that returns with the relentless pull
of a quiet, ceaseless tide.

There is a sacred breath in the half-done,
a holy unrest where the incomplete blooms
raw, unbound, alive.

The Game

Sometimes I play just to remind myself
how it feels to be unmeasured,
to leap without counting the distance.
to toss words into the wind and let them land
where they want. I hop fences in my mind,
chalk lines across hours,
hum tunes that never ask to be remembered.
I don't always want to be wise.
Sometimes, I want to be weightless,
just for a verse, just for a breath,
just long enough to become the child
I kept safe inside all this knowing.

Bloodline

My mother's voice lives in my bones
a low drum under skin and sinew
a tide of fire and whisper that rises
when the world bends too close.

Her scars are rivers beneath my flesh
mapping paths I didn't choose
but learned to walk,
each step a prayer, each breath a reckoning

I gather fragments of her storms
and quiet moments
forge them into armour
soft enough to feel, strong enough to carry forward.

In this blood I am both
the wound and the healer
an unbroken thread woven through time.

Sacred Ground

Within me lies sacred ground
where moonlight drapes the ancient stones
and whispers rise like mist
from the breath of sleeping rivers.

My flesh is earth's secret altar
where stars are sown beneath the skin
and roots of old magic coil
around the heartbeat of the soil.

I walk between worlds shadow and light
storm and stillness,
a guardian of unseen paths
that wind through body and spirit alike.

Here in the hush of my own landscape
I carry the wisdom of winds
the memory of wild rains
and the endless unfolding
of the sacred inside me.

Undertone

I carry colour the way earth keeps rust
deep, unspoken, ferrous.
A shade that holds even in shadow,
even in silence, the kind that outlasts the fire.

Archive

I am a library of unwritten lives.
Spines uncracked,
titles whispered through glass.
One is shelved in revolution,
another, in song.
Some pages smoke with fury,
some rest in dust.

I do not borrow from their silence.
I let them remain,
catalogued, named, mine.

Still, I Grow

A note from the middle ground

I no longer chase what doesn't fit.
There's a strange relief in knowing what you're not,
and letting the rest fall away without bitterness.

Growth looks different now.
It's not fire, it's embers that stay lit
even when the room goes quiet.

I learn to hold questions longer
without needing them to bloom.
To trust that some things root slowly.
That not every answer needs full light.

I still stretch, but not always upwards.
Sometimes sideways. Sometimes inward.
Sometimes I grow by staying still.

And when I falter, I don't call it failure.
I call it part of the lesson
I didn't know I needed.

Because becoming isn't a finish line.
It's the sound of your own voice
changing as you begin again,
wiser, and still
so beautifully unfinished.

Night Watch

The soul guards its fortifications
stone-thick inscrutability
archways sealed in protocol,
inner chambers braced against collapse.

I endure the day behind ramparts,
expression set in mortar,
emotion rationed as grain for siege.

Sleep unbolts the inner gate
lowering the drawbridge just enough.
Sentries of reason and restraint
gather in torchlight, their focus frayed,
a quiet game between them,
blind to what moves in the shadows.

And the spirit, unshackled, slips its captor
runs barefoot through cloisters
where memory clings to lichen
and the moat keeps its counsel in shadow.

It tiptoes through shadow,
drawn toward the warmth
breathing beneath the stone
the quiet pulse of a love condemned
that never left the keep.

NOTEBOOK EIGHT
LATITUDE OF GRACE

33°50'S, 151°12'E

Field Note on Latitude of Grace

Grace is not conferred. It is inhabited. It arrives after the long apprenticeship of return, when the self no longer disperses to meet expectation, and the body no longer yields at its fault lines. This is a latitude, not a direction. It does not chart where you are going. It marks where you have come to rest. A line held just beneath the skin, shaped by light and distance, drawn in breath and bone. Here, the self no longer leans forward to be chosen, nor folds back to be forgiven. It remains anchored, interior, intact.

At this axis, kindness moves like a current, clean and untethered. Forgiveness loosens its attachment to resolution and becomes elemental and cellular. Letting go is no longer an act of surrender but of refinement. Generosity sharpens. Tenderness holds its edge.

This notebook begins at that fixed line, somewhere south of urgency, east of need. Where the salt hangs in the air, and the horizon is steady. What follows does not rush to declare itself. It moves like water across stone, held in place by the grace it no longer has to name.

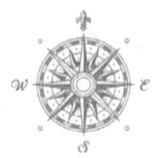

Instructions for the Next Time You Break

Let the pieces lie like ash across the root-line,
rain seeping into split earth.
Do not rush to reassemble.
Scatter, the way seeds do when the wind insists.
Lie beside something older than sorrow:
a tree that bends without yielding.
Let your breath align with its rhythm.
Let stillness reshape the outline of your name.
You are not a ruin but a cathedral
lit by a patience the sky understands.
Each fracture is a threshold.
Let the light enter.
Let the rebuilding begin in silence,
stone by deliberate stone.

Resilience

There are seasons that undo us
fracture the compass,
tilt the axis, leave the body unmoored
and the voice reaching in unfamiliar directions.

But healing, too, has coordinates.
It arrives slowly through quiet recalibrations,
the return of small rituals,
the rediscovery of stillness without collapse.

This is a chronicle of return.
to balance, to integrity,
to the interior scaffolding that held,
even when as the ground shifted.

Grace is not always given
Sometimes, we build it by hand
from the ruins of our shattering,
from the fragments we carried
through the storm.

The Pebbles

In the console: a black stone, a white one.
Each curved to the shape of thumb and thought,
each cool with intention.

I turn to them when the road begins to unravel
when I need to remember that meaning can be held
in something weightless, something worn.

The black is dense with memory,
a river-stone smoothed by long submersion.
It carries the taste of iron and ash,
a tether to what held when everything else gave way.

The white is quieter, but it hums.
Chalk-soft, a small moon at rest in my hand.
It reminds me of the space between decisions
how stillness has a texture when you pay attention.

I do not need the sky to give me signs.
Some truths ride in silence,
between the gearshift and the wheel.

This is how I move forward:
with stones beside me, dark and light,
each with a pulse I trust.

Compass

There comes a point
when you no longer need to be whole
in anyone else's language.
When you stop dimming your clarity
to ease the gaze of rooms never shaped for you.

Silence becomes a dwelling then
a deliberate form of space.
It is the slow geometry of healing,
mapped in field notes, measured in breath.

You learn to live with the cracked earth,
the unfinished pages,
the ghost maps of who you were.

And still, you place your feet,
adjust your bearings, and call the stillness
by its true name: grace.

Detachment

Grief arrived at twilight, blue-edged,
settling like dust across the room.
She sat beside me,
gathering what I could no longer carry
with the patience of leaves letting go.

Love hovered at the threshold,
light and echo trailing the scent of a fire long gone.
She made no move to enter.
Some doors remain ajar because closing them
requires a kind of death.

Memory slipped in with the wind,
earth after rain, apples just past ripe.
It stirred what I had hidden,
shook loose the floorboards
where older selves waited in silence.

Time, barefoot and relentless,
moved through me, cool river over stone
smoothing the sharpness, thinning the joy,
until everything held a strange holiness.

I stopped reaching. Listened instead
to the hush of things that remain without asking.

Now, when Loss returns, she comes through fields
smelling of turned soil and unfinished prayer.
I let her sit.

Silence stays close. And when the wind enters, I open.
What leaves, leaves. What stays, stays.
I turn again toward the sun

Ready as a field when winter has had its say.

From the Edge

By the time I understood the shape of grace,
I was no longer at the centre
but standing at the latitude
where things begin to shift.

Sacred geometry teaches:
what endures does so in pattern,
in proportion, in the unseen laws
that hold a body upright
long after its certainties fail.

Grace is the room made for breath,
for the delicate recalibration of what stays.

The Laws That Hold

I no longer measure my worth
by how much I can bear without breaking.
I have outlived the praise songs of self-erasure
the ones that called silence virtue
and named vanishing a kind of grace.

Grace, I've learned,
isn't disappearance. It is ratio.
It is the symmetry between give and keep
the architecture of restraint that does not collapse.

I live by laws not written in doctrine,
but drawn in geometry
the arc of my back unbent,
the golden mean between mercy and self.

When I am asked to explain
my refusal to unfold for convenience
I do not defend. I simply remain in alignment.
Held by principles I no longer need permission to follow.

Contour

I learned the difference between
being held and being anchored.
One arrives with weight.
The other, with atmosphere.
There are hands that bind
and hands that steady.
I have known both.

Now, I hold myself
not as something fragile,
but as a vessel fired in flame,
glazed with memory,
built to bear heat without yielding.

I move by internal bearing.
Latitude lives in the muscle.
Longitude lives in breath.
The lines that once signalled collapse
have become contour
elevation etched into silence,
held in the shape I carry.

No map required. I know the ground
by how it answers my weight.

Cartography

Loving you was never about following.
It was learning to chart a landscape
where we could walk side by side,
each carrying the weight of our own compass.
You never asked for a destination.
Just that I knew where I stood.

The Quiet Room

There is a kind of intimacy that never raises its voice.
It holds the room without claiming it,
names the moment
without carving initials into the doorframe.
This is the love that leaves no trace but peace.

Tether

Some days you are the taut line
I lean against, not to be held,
but to remember what steadiness feels like.

You don't pull. You don't yield.
You let me balance without disappearing.

Seismic Self

There was a time when your name touched my skin
like salt in a wound - sharp, necessary, unmistakable.

You marked a fault line in the lattice of my becoming.
A seismic shift etched into the compass
I now carry beneath my ribs.

Time, cartographer of the unseen,
drew new coordinates around the place
where you once lived.

The memory no longer bleeds
a trace mineral in the blood,
a residue of pain recast as wisdom.

The scar is part of the topography, but not the terrain.
The salt remains but I am not wounded.
Only tempered. Only aligned.

The Shape of Grace

Grace is not softness.
It is not the collapse into silence
nor the afterglow of apology.

It is a force held in tension,
equal and opposite
Newton's third, applied to the soul.

It is the symmetry of resilience,
missed at first glance,
but embedded in the angles of endurance.

Sacred geometry holds it,
spiral, vesica, ratio, line,
not decoration, but blueprint.

Grace is the curve
that keeps form from breaking,
the arc a bridge takes
when carrying weight without visible strain.

It is motion refined to invisibility,
A stillness perfected, deeper than surrender.

It is sovereignty coded in structure,
disciplined by choice, aligned with truth.

Gravitas

She is a lake shaped by time, unaltered by surface wind.
Depth holds its own rhythm, keeps its own counsel.

The surface shifts with weather and light,
but below, a silence forged
in seasons of bearing and release.

She gathers the broken branches,
the cast-off stories, the slow-falling griefs.
Layer by layer, they settle into form
not erased, but understood.

The world leans toward her quiet.
People pause without knowing why.
Even the birds adjust their flight as they pass over.

There is no urgency in her.
Only presence. Only the weight
of what has been tended with care for a long time.

Paper Lantern

I carry no armour, only paper
thin enough for the light
to pass through.
Held steady by quiet breath,
each moment touches softly,
illuminates gently,
the flame within visible,
alive, unshielded
by the dark.

With or Without Weather

Even on the days when the weather inside me
refuses to settle you don't ask for sun.
You wait, unmoved by the noise of my forecast,
anchored in the knowing
that I always return to calm.

Half Light

I am learning to live without the whole sky
to praise the fractured dawn,
the beauty in what opens slowly,
in what bends toward light and holds.

There is grace in the half-light
a gentler kind of knowing,
where truth settles like warmth in the hands.

Uncorrected

I no longer smooth the corners of my voice.
Let it break if it must. Let it rise without reason.

This is what it means to come home
to a version of yourself
that no longer asks to be edited.

Uncharted

I stopped asking where I was going
when I realised I already knew.

Not in the way of compass points,
but in the pulse of my breath,
the way my body leaned
toward what felt, less like fear
and more like home.

There was no map.
Just a geometry of knowing
angles remembered by muscle and silence,
coordinates marked by instinct, not ink.

I return to a version of myself
that never needed rescuing.

This is what grace does:
it rewrites the legend while keeping the terrain.
It lets you get lost, and still arrive, unscathed.

Writing the Next Thing

Even now, after long days I still write after dark.
Not because I must, but because the page
is the only place I don't explain myself.
Here, my words don't carry weight.
They carry light. Here, I build
what no one can take apart.

The Work Beneath the Work

It's never just the task. It's the way you carry it.
The way you pause before no.
The way you listen to what wasn't said.
I still walk the halls before the day begins
to feel what needs attention.
No-one notices this part.
But it's where the real work lives.

Inclination

There are angles at which the self begins to cohere.
a tuning fork struck by the quiet insistence of being.
I no longer seek arrival. Only alignment.
The body, once bent in apology,
now knows how to incline not toward permission,
but toward what is true.

Equilibrium

I have lived at the edge of almost.
Watched the self gather,
like water swelling at the lip of a dam.
This is the threshold where choice ceases to be theoretical.
And everything that has waited finally becomes real.

Sideways

It doesn't happen all at once, this returning.
First, the eyes adjust to a light that doesn't ask for endurance.
Then the body follows, no longer braced for impact.
There is no applause for survival.
Only the soft click of an internal compass realigning.
I do not rush joy.
I let it arrive as it always has
sideways, like sun on the floor
you didn't know you missed.

Laws of Return

Return is not a circle.
It is an ellipse drawn by what stayed constant
while I drifted.

There are laws for this:
every displacement carries its own correction,
every orbit, a hunger for coherence.

I do not come back to reclaim what was.
I return to honour the arc
to step again into the silence that remembered me
when I had forgotten my own name.

Meridian

There are lines we cross without knowing
a threshold of forgiveness,
an internal equator where grief gives way
to something else.

I walked that line.
No final word, no clean break.
Only the steady shift from ache to air.

I name it now as latitude
a measure not of place,
but of possibility.

Golden Mean

Nature arranges in ratio
the spiral of shell, the unfolding fern,
the curve that carries memory forward
without breaking its line.

I look for that symmetry in myself,
a quiet reckoning between origin and becoming,
growth that does not abandon its root,
movement measured not in speed, but in grace.

Tesseract

I once believed things were flat
that sorrow passed in straight lines,
that grace arrived as light across a surface.

But beyond the cube lies another dimension:
a shadow of the infinite, cast into the confines of form.

I glimpse it sometimes: the way memory bends,
how forgiveness curves back on itself,
how what feels final was never the edge.

There is structure inside the unseen
fold upon fold, a depth shaped by what we almost missed.
And in that folding, grace reveals itself
as space opening inward.

Equinox

This is the season
where day and night stand level
not in peace, but in tension.

The earth tilts, but keeps its poise.
I learn from this
how to hold my own dark without apology,
how to let light come without permission.

Equilibrium, I am learning,
is not stillness but motion
done with care.

Perimeter

There are boundaries I no longer explain.
The grace I practice now is architectural:
load-bearing, spatial,
a kind of geometry
that requires nothing extra to stand.
If I have become a structure you cannot enter,
know this: it is not a fortress. It is a frame.

Caliper

Some mornings I become the measuring tool.
Jaw set to tension, I gauge the distance
between who I am and who I should have been.

No one asks, but I answer in corrected sentences,
in glances smoothed to neutrality.

The mind keeps score in units too small to speak aloud:
an eyebrow lifted, a delay in praise,
the sting of almost disguised as grace.

I move through the day like steel on stone
exact, unfinished, searching for the point
where pressure equals worth.

Even in sleep I do the math.
Dream in fractions.
Wake with the ache of miscalculation.

Laughter, Sums, and Stuff
Field notes on gravity and eggs

He speaks of gravity the way a farmer speaks of soil
with the weight of someone who has fallen into it
and risen again.

"*Sums and stuff*", he says, as if saying grace:
his voice balancing the equation
between laughter and the unspeakable.

He does not solve the world. He names it,
one broken law of motion at a time.

His hands sketch the curve of time
into a dish towel,
folds the known and unknown
into the same drawer.

He tells me the universe is expanding over eggs -
the yolk a sun, spinning lightly on the edge of silence.

He is not a man of certainties.
He walks the fine line between proof and wonder
and still finds joy where the numbers end.

Quantum things, he calls them.
Particles, probability, the ache of being split and whole.
Somehow, he lives among them
without needing to be right.

His laughter makes a cathedral of the kitchen.
A theory of joy, written in coffee rings
and the steam on morning glass.

And each day, he does not lift the world
he simply steadies it, makes space

for small questions to stay unanswered
without shame.

Fetch

You were barefoot,
throwing the ball again
the dogs tearing after it,
shoulders low,
bodies all velocity and joy.

I stood in the doorway
half-shadowed, half-pretending I wasn't watching.
Your arm rose and fell,
a metronome measuring out the dusk
each motion its own quiet purpose,
unaware of being held in my gaze.

Something in me, tight for so long, unclenched.
Recognition moved through me
like breath remembered after holding it too long.

You looked up, as if sensing the shift.
already past the point of turning back,
I only said, *"They'll never stop if you keep throwing it."*

You laughed. But I didn't.
I was too full of the truth that had just found its name.

Anchor Point

It isn't always a location.
Sometimes the anchor is a choice
repeated in silence until it becomes shape.

The body remembers the centre
long before the mind agrees.
Not a compass. Not a flare.
Something quieter,
the weight of standing still when the tide pulls
every other version of you out to sea.
It steadies in the unspoken.
The name you carry inward.
The place you do not leave
even when everything else begins to drift.

Continuance

There is no final word. Only the shifting of light
across a surface we thought was fixed.
Only the slow realisation that healing is not an ending
but a new kind of precision.

What breaks does not always collapse.
Sometimes it becomes the shape we grow around.
Sometimes it teaches us how to bend without apology.

This is not closure.
This is latitude: the measured widening
of what the body can carry and still remain upright.
The recalibration of truth within the self.

I no longer name myself by what was lost,
but by what stayed:
the quiet resolve, the creative flame,
the trace of salt no longer wounding,
only seasoning.

I remember the fault lines
to understand the architecture they revealed.
I do not smooth them out.
I map around them.
build their memory into the mortar.

I belong now to no one's version but my own.
My centre is not still, but steady.
I am my own axis and found, at last,
that grace was never above or beyond me
but emanating from within all along.

NOTEBOOK NINE
AZIMUTH

43.7696° N, 11.2558° E

Field Note on Azimuth and the Arc of Return

Some returns are revisions, an arc drawn back across familiar ground, read now from higher elevation. The original path remains, but the perspective has changed. What once felt fractured reveals its contour. The terrain that once disoriented begins to resolve.

To cross the line of return is not to begin again, but to re-enter with the kind of knowing that only distance affords. You arrive at the same coordinates, but the self that stands there has altered. What was once uncertain is now rendered in contour: ridgelines, descents, and plateaus all part of the same shape.

The terrain itself has not shifted. What has changed is your azimuth, your angle of orientation, the internal calibration that determines what you see and what you move toward. It is a subtle redirection, but it alters everything. This is not a return to origin. It is a return with reference. A bearing drawn not from where you began, but from how far you've travelled, and how precisely you've learned to hold the line.

You carry no map now, only the memory of ascent, and the feel of the instrument in your hand, the steady pull of the horizon, and the knowledge that you are aligned. Not by accident. By design.

Florence

(Somewhere just North of grace)

North of grace, terracotta dawn deepens,
arching rooftops exhale,
balconies breathe linen into the burnished air.

Florence speaks in lines long drawn,
streets tracing sketches my body once knew,
steps unfolding a self sketched in sandstone and shadow.

Silence speaks my name, a voice vivid, unadorned
marble gazes meeting mine through myth and matter,
stone eyes that summon, pulling presence from the marrow.

Here, truth surfaces slowly, a breath breaking free,
light layering stone until each contour carves clarity.

And in this latitude an older self rises,
awake, aligned, and anchored
in her own becoming.

Sovereignty

I unfasten the harness of borrowed expectations,
shake loose the shadows others cast upon my soul
chains forged from softer metals,
gilt but brittle, shaped by hands
I no longer recognise.

Heartbreak has no throne here;
its dominion fractured, its maps redrawn
in a language of my choosing.
Control retreats, defeated by the slow uprising
of breath, blood, bone
my pulse a sovereign rhythm,
beating boldly, fiercely free.

I reclaim sacred ground:
of soul, a country unmapped,
of voice, a law unwritten,
of strength forged from scars,
of dignity seared into sinew,
each wound worn as wisdom,
each grief ground into grit.

This is the place I call my own
autonomous, absolute,
ruled by no hand but my own heart's decree.
Here, in the marrow of freedom,
I am the architect, the anthem,
the unvanquished land.

Mosaic

I am made of fractured porcelain
shards gathered tenderly,
edges softened by fingers
that no longer fear sharpness.
In these broken tesserae,
imperfection finds voice,
each crack singing softly
of gravity and grace.

My flaws wear no apology;
they thread my seams with gold,
every fissure lit from within
veins of sunlight coursing through stone.
Mistakes become maps, wounds deepen into wells
each scar a silent spring feeding roots beneath skin.

Here stands the woman built from fragments and fire,
reclaimed, remade, beauty bound not in symmetry
only bold impermanence
a peace found in imperfect wholeness,
every broken edge held lovingly
within the trembling hands of acceptance.

Absolution

I open my palms releasing memory like smoke
ashes lifting gently, drifting free from embers
I refuse to stir again.

My heart unhooks its tether,
softening knots long tightened
by sorrow's silent fingers.

Forgiveness rises, an incense of cedar and sage
cleansing old wounds,
washing bitterness from my veins.
I unname every ache, whispering release
into air sweetened by grace's quiet bloom.

Those who wronged me I unbind from my bones,
returning their shadows to a twilight that no longer
shapes my waking hours.
I surrender resentment to rivers deep enough
to carry it gently into seas of mercy.

My heart lifts, a feather untangled from thorns
finally free, breathing fully
in the sanctuary of absolution.

Dream Archive

They come unbidden,
shards of light and shadow,
stitched together in the loom behind the mind.

A staircase that leads nowhere.
A voice without a mouth.
The sea rising in a room you thought was safe.

In sleep, rules are rewritten:
gravity forgets its grip, time folds like paper,
and you speak to the dead
as if no silence stands between.

Some dreams are maps
drawn in ash and honey
you wake tasting longing,
unable to name what you almost remembered.

Others vanish like dew in first light
truths too soft for daylight to bear.

Still, we return each night to that strange cathedral
of flicker and hum,
trusting that even our illusions
are trying to tell us something.

The Quiet Beneath

I went looking for silence,
not the absence of sound
but the presence of stillness
a hush that holds, not empties.

It did not come in the shape I expected
no mountaintop, no ocean sigh.
Just the soft cadence of breath
uncoiling inside me.

Peace was not a prize but a place I cleared
stone by stone, story by story,
until the ground stopped trembling.

Now I walk without reaching.
The world is not quieter,
only kinder and I am part of its rhythm,
not its resistance.

Sanctuary

Sagrada Família, 41.4036° N, 2.1744° E

Sunlight streamed through the nave in long gold blades
cutting shadow clean from stone.

Above me, sunflowers blazed across the ceiling.
Too bright for sorrow, too deliberate to ignore.

And then it rose, not memory, but force
as if her absence had finally found its way back
through the body.

No image, no whisper,
just the heat behind the breastbone
and the unmistakable knowing: she was near.

I stood very still, but inside something collapsed,
quietly, completely.

When the sobs came, they came as release,
years of restraint spilled in cathedral air.

A stranger beside me took my hand
without hesitation a Spanish woman,
unknown, unnamed.

She held on with the steadiness of someone
who had also loved and lost.
And in her silence, my mother became presence.

The sunflowers did not dim.
They turned toward me as if I were light.
As if I still belonged to the living.

David

Galleria dell'Accademia, Florence

43.7696° latitude, 11.2558° longitude

I thought I'd be unmoved.
Another icon. Another crowd.
Another body carved into certainty.

But he was taller than silence.
And still. Not heroic, human.
The curve of the spine still listening to burden,
hands too large for peace.

He wasn't waiting to strike.
He was waiting to decide.
And that was what broke me.

The softness in the jaw.
The furrow not yet turned to wrath.
The vein pulsing in stone as if blood were possible.

I had not expected to find grace
in a figure so known.
But there it was: poise without arrogance,
youth holding what it did not yet understand.

And I, stripped of defences, stood in the flood of it.
Remembering how beauty, unasked for, undoes.

The Cartographer's Return

I unrolled what remained - creased parchment,
stained with past weather.
No legend, only the imprint of rivers
that altered course in silence.

I moved through undergrowth of absence
each step a negotiation between memory and stone.
Here, a ridge of restraint.
There, a clearing where something once yielded.

I made no marks. Let the terrain instruct me.
Listened to the grain of the path,
the lean of branches, the hush where wind
once faltered.

In that hush, I found a new axis.
in the slow alignment of breath and bearing.

To love again is a return to unmapped ground
still shifting, still alive
and the discipline of moving through it
with my heart open.

Torso

41.8933° N, 12.4829° E

She stands where light slants through a clerestory,
dust caught mid-air like breath withheld.

No label, no cordon, just the austerity
of stone worn to truth
arm sheared at the shoulder,
mouth half-formed, hip split clean
along a stress line older than empires.

Still, she anchors the room.

And I, still not fluent in the shape I've become
stood in her orbit long enough to feel it shift.

No prayer passed between us,
only the quiet charge of recognition
the way one body knows another by its fracture.

She did not offer solace. She did not turn.
But in the exact geometry of what remained,
I found the grammar of endurance
a syntax that required no restoration.

San Marco

5.4408° latitude, 12.3155° longitude

Salt air peeled at the paint.
Ropes creaked softly.
Somewhere behind me,
a shutter closed like breath.

I wandered past the same blue door
three times before realising I wasn't lost.
I just wasn't going anywhere in particular.

In a chapel, a violin note refused to end.
So I stayed until it did. Because I could.

The Eternal City

41.9028° latitude, 12.4964° longitude

My feet ached.
The map tore in my pocket.
I sat on a curb
and ate figs with my fingers.

In a church, a child lit a candle
with too much joy for the quiet.
No one scolded her.

I walked the Forum at dusk.
Didn't try to imagine the past.
It was enough that everything broken
still stood.

Marrow

Some loves rearrange us: not in the breaking,
but in the slow shift of bone toward what holds.

They do not conquer. They align.
Drawing us inward
without pressure, without sound.

This isn't the story of falling.
It is the record of choosing,
of stepping, full-weighted,
into the open field
knowing it may not hold.

To love like this is not to be kept.
It is to enter with reverence,
to move in orbit,
and leave the center undisturbed
when the closeness dissolves.

What remains is a line, invisible, magnetic,
a return path drawn through marrow,
for the soul that once dared
to go all the way in.

Montmartre

48.8566° latitude, 2.3522° longitude

The Seine moved like wet ink,
and I followed it past shuttered bookstalls,
past the gaze of stone saints who'd seen too much.

I stood before Degas:
ballerinas mid-turn, elegant and exhausted.
I saw myself, not graceful, but enduring.

Later, in Montmartre, I painted my lips red.
A woman alone on Rue des Martyrs,
buying raspberries for no reason but joy.

And in that small act, something returned.
not youth, not permission,
but presence - whole, and fully mine.

Sieve

34.6682° latitude, 20.2300° longitude

The world pours through me
faster than I can hold it:
Grief, pattern, colour,
the raw edge of newsprint,
a glance I didn't expect to carry.

So I shape what remains,
what clings to the wire
after the water runs clear.

It is never the whole story.
Only what resists being forgotten.
Only what insists on staying.

Convergence

-33.8486° latitude, 151.2131° longitude

You looked up and the air rethreaded itself
around your stillness, a fulcrum
the atmosphere had long been waiting for.
I knew the shift before it registered
in the tilt of breath,
how my spine realigned without command.

The bone deep correction of a trajectory
too long adrift.
Years had taught me to travel light,
to orbit without anchoring.
But something in your gravity rewrote the path
with such calibrated certainty:
the event horizon of recognition
a geometry resolved
in the silence between fixed points.

Customs

55.6761° latitude, 12.5683° longitude

No one asked why my passport was newly issued.
No one weighed the silence I carried in my carry-on.

I walked foreign streets a woman relearning her name.
Ordered wine in the language of risk.
Sat alone without explanation or apology.

Ruins made sense, the beauty of what remains
when the original plan is gone.

And somewhere between
arrival gate and cathedral stone,
I stopped bracing for absence.
I belonged to my own itinerary.

Not healed. Not whole.
But finally on my way.

Provenance

I aligned with nothing fixed,
no angle imposed, no theorem proved.
You moved through me radius to arc,
unmeasured, yet true.
To love again is to draw the shape
that draws itself
form held by intention alone.

The Language We Spoke

We never named it.
What passed between us lived outside grammar
measured not in nouns but in intervals.
You found me the way a compass finds north
not directly, but with reverence for the arc.
We spoke in constellations, half-glances,
the sacred geometry of nearness.
And when I turned to speak,
you were already listening
to more than my voice
but to the thoughts beneath it.

First Response

Your smile caught me mid-motion
hand raised, thought forming,
already halfway through the moment I thought I was in.
It didn't beckon. It didn't soothe.
It hit like a signal; clear, deliberate,
wired straight to the chest where logic faltered
and instinct lit a flare.
Everything sharpened: the noise, the colour,
even the space between us.
I stood inside the impact,
breathless like something rare
had entered the atmosphere
and left its mark before I could name it.

Contact

You smiled, and something in me
forgot how to behave like a body,
the rhythm I'd worn all day splintered in recognition.

Just that tilt of your mouth,
like you knew a secret
you had no intention of keeping.

My breath stuttered, my thoughts scattered
pages loose in a sudden wind.

And you, still mid-conversation,
still unaware of the small, irreversible
collision you'd caused.

Risky Business

Loving you means stepping beyond the known equation
past the perimeter I'd drawn in chalk
around my own becoming.

It didn't feel like falling.
It felt like entering a new system of motion,
where mass bent space, and tenderness had gravity.

You didn't ask for belief.
You simply stood, constant,
unaccelerated - and I,
like an object seeking the most elegant path,
moved toward you without resistance.

There are no formulas for what we risk
when we yield to love.
Only the quiet miracle of reconfiguration.

Euclidean Quiet

Love came in symmetry
the way you passed the mug
with both hands, how your silence
was never a void but a held space.

You knew where to stand in a room that was mine,
without rearranging the furniture.

We spoke in angles, the soft alignment
of small gestures, a choreography unnoticed by others.

This is the love I believe in
the kind that hums just beneath the threshold of sound,
constant as the laws that keep us upright.

Even Then

Even knowing how the story folds
its fracture lines, its silence
I would still step into you.

Still offer the entirety of my breath,
the unguarded map of my interior.

Because for a time, you were the singularity
dense, luminous, pulling me past
what I thought I could survive.

I crossed the event horizon
without knowing whether I'd return,
only that I had found something vast enough
to change my coordinates.

And though time dilated,
and the world around me slowed,
I did not regret the gravity of loving you.

Chiaroscuro

You entered my life the way light reclaims a wall
without moving a thing,
yet shifting everything into clarity.

I saw more because your presence
revealed the contours
I had taught myself to overlook.

You were never the flame.
You were the frame in which contrast found meaning,
where shadow earned its shape.

And I, drawn to the architecture of your attention,
learned that love doesn't always blaze.
Sometimes it's a window, open just enough
to let the truth fall in.

Intaglio

I didn't count the hours.
There was no ledger, no index of gestures
to prove what passed between us.

But I remember the weight of your hand
when it rested beside mine
not touching, just present.
A line drawn in negative space.

These are the marks that stay:
the grain of your voice when it caught
on something unspoken,
the lift of breath before you left a room.

I loved you the way I was taught to see
in subtle relief, in quiet contours
of light and shadow
where symmetry dissolves into something gentler
and more true.
What remains is inscription. Invisible from afar,
revealed only to the careful tracing of fingertips

Flare

It struck mid-stride as fire
breaking skin from the inside.
My ribs lit first, then the throat
a flicker too whole to be named.
Laughter rose, unbidden,
from the architecture of my own survival.
It moved through tendon and scar
like heat that had always belonged.
Just the flare of undiminished joy.

Longitude

You stand where the longitudes cross
stone underfoot, sky split to measure.
Between us, a strip of ground
worn smooth by looking
at the weight of what remains unsaid.
I read the line you draw, as law.
Space does its work, undistracted and exact.
Even my ribs adjust around it,
aware of your shape without seeking contact.
What I feel travels under the skin
a current with no demand
held in the geometry between presence and restraint

Axiomatically You

You were the undeniable presence
everything leaned toward you.
Like trees in wind they've learned to trust.

You were not force. You were mass.
Not the kind that overwhelms,
but the kind that calibrates
steadies the field without needing to speak.

I had studied this in other forms
the symmetry of stillness,
the law that governs orbit without touch.

You never asked to be known.
But I knew you like an axiom a truth I couldn't explain,
only feel until everything else aligned around it.

Saltwork

What remains is the salt
left in the seams of worn fabric,
crusting the edge of thought.

I move forward by residue
what the body casts off in effort,
what memory dries into evidence.

There are no signs,
only the grain of things
once tasted, once endured.

Salt keeps what the rest forgets
a crust along the collarbone,
white as bone dust,
proof that I was there.

Ratio

We were golden, not flawless,
but proportioned.
Moments unfolding like spirals in nature:
unexpected, yet exactly as they should be.

I carried you the way a painter
lays down under-drawing
scarcely visible, but necessary
for the structure to hold.

And though I know what came after the glitch,
the falter in the sequence,
I still return, sometimes, to that early geometry
where everything fit,
only to remember how it felt to move inside a living ratio.

Arch

Loving you is never chaos.
It is design, a span across absence,
a curve drawn to carry what words could not.

I didn't know I was building
until I stepped back and saw the symmetry,
how even longing can form structure
if given the right tension.

You are the keystone.
Not weightless, but exact,
not the centre, but the point
that makes everything hold.

I love you the way
my father taught me to see structure:
in shadow, in balance,
in what stays upright when the feeling leaves.
Even now, I move beneath what we built,
an arch standing quietly, holding its shape.

Grammar of Light

I paint to ask questions the mouth cannot hold.

Light spills differently each day.
I follow its declension across the wall,
conjugate colour into comprehension.

Some mornings, a shadow breaks open
what logic stitched shut.
And I understand something
by naming its reflection on stone.

Palimpsest

I never spoke the words.
Some things fracture what they try to name.
What moves between us
lives in the grain beneath language,
a breath too charged to speak,
held in ink that never sets.

We write ourselves in half-gestures,
in the press of thought stalled at the skin.
Your mouth shapes what never arrives,
and still I read it.

Time layers over what once was clear.
But under each revision,
the first inscription holds
pressure left in the fibres,
script scored too deep to forget.

Even now, I trace the faint strokes
with the body's memory
a truth rubbed thin but never erased.

Recalibration

The city remains but the coordinates have shifted.
Same pavement. Same fractured curb beneath the Jacaranda.
Yet everything leans differently now.

You altered the interior topography with presence.
A shift in magnetic field, subtle as breath,
but enough to turn the needle.

That café window still reflects me,
but slightly off-centre as if some echo of you
refracts through glass I never touched.

You weren't a destination. You were deviation.
The unplotted arc that redrew my axis
without permission or regret.

I still navigate the same streets,
but nothing aligns as it once did.
And even now, I orient toward
that imperceptible curve you left in the map.

Cartography

You didn't chart me.
You studied, like a field naturalist
waiting for the animal
to appear on its own terms.

I had drawn borders in places I'd forgotten,
territories marked by what I would not name.

You never asked.
You stayed long enough
for the terrain to speak.

Not once did you redraw me.
You let the shape hold.
And in your patience,
something shifted.

I had been a map folded too tightly.
And in your hands, the creases softened.

Joinery

There is relief in building something.
A sentence, a chair, a sketch that holds.

I do not begin with vision
only with the ache to place one piece
beside another until the world stops splintering.

A line becomes a joint, a phrase, a brace.
This is not escape. It is structure.

It is how I remain upright.

Penumbra

You do not haunt me. You hover.
Not as ghost, but as contour
a softened edge in the periphery of thought.

I don't speak your name aloud.
I trace it internally,
the arc of a sun just below the horizon.

What remains isn't grief.
It's the part of love
that outlasts the architecture of nearness
without touch, the held breath
between pulse and retreat.

Some truths don't disappear.
They diffuse.
You are no longer the centre,
but the light that bends quietly
around what's left.

Threshold

There was a moment I could have stepped back
remained in the safety of the known pattern.
But you stood still, without questions
or promises, only presence.

No script. No questions.
Just a quiet opening wide enough to walk through.

I crossed it. Without certainty,
but a kind of holy inexactitude,
the way light enters through stained glass:
fragmented, but utterly committed.

And now, no matter what followed,
the line remains as blessing:
the place where I once chose
to love with the whole of my weight.

Stonefruit

Love has a pit - hard, central,
something you bite around.
It stains the hands if held too long,
sweet, until the bruise makes itself known.
We reach for it because the taste reminds us
we are capable of ripening.

Continuum

Let this stand as record: I loved you.
It was never your light I followed,
but the dim between your questions,
the way your voice thinned
when the day wore too long.

If I never speak it again,
it is not silence made from shame, but reverence.
Some truths are thinned by too much naming.

Still, they remain.
This one settles deep, in the marrow,
quiet as a tide pulling beneath still water.
Steady as the hum that lingers after
a song you thought had finished.

You are no longer my breath.
But you are a line I carry
threaded through quiet, unbroken, and intact.

Echo Chamber

Regret is the sound that returns
after the latch has closed.
Not sharp, just steady. A low fidelity ache,
looping beneath what's been left unsaid.

It speaks in edits: what should have braced,
what failed to hold, the pause too long,
the word misaligned.

The final sentence replays with new inflection each time.
Meaning shifts depending on the wall it hits.
No answer. Only reverb.
A voice turned back on itself,
searching for a version that won't come.

Index

You won't find it in the prologue.
It lives in the footnotes,
the breath held before the page turns,
the margin where fingers brush mid-sentence.

Love isn't the story, it's the index.
The way your name appears
in chapters you never touched,
threaded through moments
you didn't mean to enter.
It doesn't ask for authorship.
Only presence. Only the quiet pattern of return.

You

You are the singularity the point of no return
where all knowing narrowed into presence,
where time bent inward and the past threaded itself
through the same seam
the future was already passing.
I crossed into you with no promise of exit.
It wasn't that I didn't know better
but because I finally did.

Cutting Stone

I come to the page as a mason approaches stone:
to strike at what resists its own naming.
The work is never clean.
It blisters, splinters, leaves dust in the lungs.
But in the fault lines, something truer takes shape.
I do not seek beauty.
I listen for the sound a line makes
when it fits, the click of form meeting intention.
This is pilgrimage: a return to the source
beneath the noise, beneath even language.

Matriarch

I have learned to live with the gravity of elephants
to carry what matters, to remember in my marrow
what the world would rather forget.

There are paths I never marked, yet my feet know them.
Tracks laid long before me
by women who walked with quiet conviction,
pressing memory into earth.

I carry the weight of what came before
grief softened into guidance, history turned shelter,
strength shaped by time and tenderness.

I walk wide and deliberate,
each step an offering for those who follow.
The rhythm is mine now
earned, steady, deep as drumbeat.

I lead because the path opened.
I stayed because the water was needed.
Presence became direction.
Steadiness became song.

This life holds depth.
It holds ache and meaning in equal measure.
And I have learned to move with all of it.

I am the map, the landmark,
the legacy still becoming.

Someone will come,
a daughter, a woman with questions,
a soul shaped by weather
and she will find the path
by the way the ground feels sure beneath her feet.

Axis

You walked through every room of me
hallway, attic, unlit corridors
I had sealed with silence.

Not to rearrange, but to dwell.
To see how the light moved differently
through my architecture.

There was no threshold you avoided.
No locked drawer you did not rest your hand upon
without prying.

I who had once only offered fragments let you in.
What we built did not last.
But the frame remains. The centre still holds
because I loved at full rotation.

And for once, I did not orbit.
I became my own axis.

Keel

They think strength lives in the mast,
in the sail, in what's seen.

But I am the keel, submerged,
steady as breath held beneath the surface.

I do not rise. I resist drift.
When the wind thrashes,
when the hull groans,
I cut deep through the dark
and hold course.

Let them claim the horizon.
I'll take the weight, the salt, the silent pull
that keeps everything upright.

Mercy

Some mornings, you lift the day before the sun does
not because you're ready,
but because someone needs you to.

You become the still point,
the hand that doesn't tremble,
the voice that steadies,
even as something unnamed
quivers in your own chest.

No-one sees the quiet scaffolding you become
the way your backbone bends
to brace the grief of others,
the way your silence becomes shelter.

You keep going because love has its own geometry
a kind of architecture that holds even when cracked.

And in the hollow of the night,
when the house breathes evenly
and no one is watching,
you finally let your breath shake
the smallest mercy in a day that asked for strength
without pause.

NOTEBOOK TEN
SINGULARITY

90°00'00"S

Field Note on Singularity

Here, at the axis where all meridians meet, there is no direction left, only convergence. No north, no east, no future shaped by horizon. Only this still, unshadowed point beneath the turning sky, where latitude holds and movement no longer defines.

This is the nature of singularity: it draws everything inward and compacts it into substance. Former shapes lose their edges and fold into one another, forming something that cannot be separated or undone. The self no longer scatters across ash and bone. It no longer thins in the drift or dissolves in the softness of forgetting. What remains is core pressed by time, clarified by pressure, and made durable by everything it has endured. It does not waver. It holds. It carries the full weight of its own name.

You are not arriving. You have already crossed the threshold, what follows now is consolidation. You are no longer becoming, you are setting. The shape holds. The change cannot be undone. The map ends here, but the meaning doesn't vanish. It compacts. It crystallises. Every fault line absorbed. Every arc resolved. Grace no longer stretches outward. It coheres. You do not stand at the centre. You are the condition through which centre is defined. Not a fixed point on the compass, but the gravity that holds it in place. This is singularity: the self drawn to its most exact dimension, unmapped, unreplicated, whole.

True North

I no longer measure direction by distance.
It's a matter of alignment
how thought meets intention,
how breath settles into the shape of choice.

Some coordinates are not discovered,
only returned to in the body,
in the rhythm that remains
when striving stops.

This is a knowing not sought,
but inherited from silence.
Not the map, the magnet beneath it.

The Architecture of Joy

I designed it deliberately room by room:
this load-bearing joy - not decorative, necessary.

There were decisions about scale
how much space one needs
to stand without apology,
how light should enter
without interrogation.

The foundation was repetition.
The walls, a refusal to measure myself
by what could be taken.

There is symmetry in choosing
what does not collapse
under the weight of one's own name.

This is not a sanctuary.
It is a structure.
And I live here now, on purpose.

Suture

There are things I stitched closed too early
wounds not ready, truths still wet
with their first admission.

I thought healing meant hiding
and mastering the art of appearing whole.

But shame seeps through clean seams.
It rises in the throat like undone thread,
a slow fray of everything I tried to control.

There is grace in the re-opening.
Even the raw can be honest.

Cartography

I make maps because the terrain keeps shifting.
Not to find a way out,
but to understand where the edges hold.

Some truths only reveal themselves in graphite,
in the rhythm of line chasing
the shape of a thing that won't stand still.

The page becomes country.
A border forms here, a fault line cracks there.
I press until patterns emerge
contours rising gently,
edges mapping the terrain of what could be.

Lexicon of the Hand

It begins in the wrist, a shift, a signal,
meaning rising through muscle before language wakes.

It travels bone to tendon, etching urgency into skin.
There is no blueprint, only the need to make.

Sometimes it scorches. Sometimes it carves.
Always, it calls. I name it grammar
the hand's way of speaking what the soul cannot hoard.

Superposition

I no longer ask the sky to hold still.
I've learned to read movement
without mistaking it for instability.

Certainty was a younger hunger
the impulse to name what could already be felt,
to bind truth to a fixed position.

But meridians drift. Latitude adjusts.
Light arrives at fractional angles
and still the day begins.

The arrow of time no longer threatens.
It offers no direction toward conclusion,
but through expansion.

And I, not anchored, but aligned
continue under open sky, unmapped, but exact.

Parallax

I see more from here
the view unchanged,
yet I am shifted.
This is the gift of movement:
a fresh angle,
a wider scope.

I have come to trust the geometry of shift
the arc that widens without breaking form,
a radius drawn from an unseen centre that holds.

I do not need the world to stay still
to understand it.

Some truths emerge only in orbit
when time and position align
just long enough to reveal
what was always there.

Particle and Wing

I am not one thing. Never was.
Some days I move as line
clear, directional, cutting clean across
what asks to be known.
Other days, I expand
a presence without outline,
felt more than seen.
It's not contradiction.
It's form, depending on what meets me.
A kind of loyalty to both edge and atmosphere.
I've let go of needing to collapse
into one version.
Light doesn't. Why should I?

Inner Physics

What steadies me now isn't faith or stillness.
It's bone-marrow-deep, salt-lined
the quiet structure
that doesn't shift just because I do.
I've stopped measuring what can't be seen.
Some forces are felt in the dust long after they've passed.
Bone, salt, milk, dust
what I'm made of, what stays.
I carry it without question.
Without noise.
The weight of barefooted innocence.

Vector Mind

My mind works in motion,
not speed, but trajectory.
Each thought carries mass,
each decision a vector
with direction and weight.

I don't gather answers.
I chart momentum,
follow how questions arc
before they land.

I work in tension
between impulse and pause,
between what pulls
and what must be held.

This is load-bearing logic,
refined through resistance,
corrected by impact.

What I know doesn't sit still.
It balances, shifts,
adjusts its stance
to meet the weight
of what comes next.

90° South

At the bottom of the world,
you reach the place where striving ends.
Every direction is north there is nowhere left to run.

Here, the wind does not chase.
It shapes what stands still.
Light circles without ascent,
returning each day to itself.

Lines of longitude converge, revealing a quieter strength:
the grace of holding position, the steady courage
of remaining anchored
exactly where you are.
This is the centre,
where motion gives way to presence,
where becoming means
standing wholly in your place.

There is no edge to cross. No path to trace.
Only the stark geometry of staying,
and the quiet power of knowing it is enough.

Finale: Singularity

You learn not to measure a life in milestones,
but in the fault lines you crossed without breaking
the asymmetries you named as balance.

There is no fixed geometry for becoming.
Only what the body remembers:
the tensile grace of thresholds,
the golden ratio of what was given
and what you chose to keep.

You were not unbroken. You were exact.
Aligned by the quiet mathematics of what endured.

There came a point, precise as light tipping across a threshold
when you no longer translated yourself
into other people's syntax.
When your voice stopped curving to fit the room.

You no longer feared your singularity.
You stepped into it, a collapse into self,
into gravity, into the field
where time bent inward and left you fully known.

It is return to the arrow of time
as it carves forward through you.
To the aperture that was never a wound, but a portal.

You carry no doctrine only the coordinates of grace,
the symmetry of having once remained
with what was breaking,
And finally, called it yours.

Epilogue

For My Children, When I Am Gone

I don't live to be remembered.
I live to bear witness
to beauty that outlasts reason,
and the quiet strength of staying.
I leave no map.
Only the trace of how I move through this world:
eyes open, feet steady,
heart full - even when cracked.

I was never the fire, I was the flint.
What I built had splinters,
sharp edges, a pulse.
I do not leave you perfection.
I leave you something truer:
a life made by choice, by courage,
by the daily act of showing up.

What I leave is the rhythm of my voice
when you doubt yourself,
the knowing that you are loved
without condition, without pause.

My legacy is not a name.
It is a field where the stubborn things grow,
where sorrow blooms beside the wheat.
What I planted was meant to feed
the hungry places in us.

And if the world turns cold, and it will, remember this:
I am here. I am yours.
You are not a chapter. You are the story.
The root and the reason.
The North Star that keeps me true.

Loving you is not what I once did,
it is what I do with every breath,
and every turning of the sky.

www.ingramcontent.com/pod-product-compliance
Lightning Source LLC
Chambersburg PA
CBHW032040200426
43209CB00049B/49